this book and get ready to expand your mind, your abilities, and your overall awesomeness!"

— Tyler Tichelaar, Ph.D. and award-winning author of *Spirit of the North: A Paranormal Romance*

"Meredith Herrenbruck's *Becoming Ridiculously Awesome*, besides having one of the greatest book titles ever in the history of publishing, offers a great roadmap to improve or recreate your life no matter where you are in your life's journey. Taking a holistic approach, Herrenbruck offers a well-rounded guide to help you bring out your awesomeness physically, mentally, spiritually, and emotionally. It offers great perspective based on her own journey as well as the journey of others she's met and worked with over the years. The book includes numerous exercises designed to help you bring out your awesome, provided you take the time to complete them. Finally, and quite awesomely, preceding each chapter is a rune Herrenbruck shares that illustrates the concept covered in the chapter. Fans of symbology will love what this book shares, bringing ancient knowledge from the past into the present and helping us to use ancient wisdom to solve contemporary challenges we face today. Bravo to Meredith Herrenbruck on this fresh take to the personal development genre!"

— Jonathan Wong, MBA, M.Ed., MPA and author of *Succeeding in College and Life, Driving Profits and Making Bank,* and *Tales from Behind the Wheel: Year One*

"Every time I work with you, Meredith, I have profound insights, my heart heals, and I feel better about myself or just have better reactions to others, which helps while being a daughter, sister, wife, and mother. My perspective on problems shifts so dramatically every time I do a session. Thank you, Meredith; you are an angel, and life keeps getting better and better since we started working together."

— Anne M., San Francisco, CA

"For those prepared to live the life they were truly meant to live, this empowering and wise guide will show you how to leave behind being stuck and enter the portal into a life of freedom and joy."

— Cinthia Dennis, author of *Seasons of the Heart: A Guide for Girls about Love, Dating and Boys*

"Becoming Ridiculously Awesome provides a step-by-step, holistic approach that allows your true unique self to develop. The book is full of wonderful prompts, exercises, and inspirational stories, aided by Meredith's sharing of her own easy-to-relate-to experiences."

— Kim Chamberlain, Author & Speaker, New Zealand

"Meredith is ridiculously awesome! Her years of knowledge, skill, and insight are woven together beautifully in her new book Becoming Ridiculously Awesome. Meredith's (constellation) work is extraordinary, and she navigates complex family and ancestral dynamics and patterns with great skill and awareness, which allows her clients to transform their feelings of "stuckness." She can help you change your life, heal, grow, and learn more about your life purpose. You won't be disappointed."

— Lisa Redstone, M.A.

"This book is transformational! I loved it! If you want to make better choices to move forward to greater success in your life, this book is for you. Meredith weaves together mental, physical, and spiritual ideas and shares with you how to get unstuck and learn how to make positive changes to achieve your goals. She walks with you every step of the way. Thank you, Meredith!"

— Penny Rempfer, Ed.D., Transformational Coach & CEO of Dr. Penny Rempfer Coaching and Consulting, Woodinville, WA

"As someone who has also taken a similar, yet very different, journey to find enlightenment I found myself on the edge of my seat as I was reading...wondering what new tool or experience Meredith was going to share next. I think that, as light workers, sometimes we need confirmation of our experiences as our soul is vast and often these experiences can be rather odd or otherworldly and understanding another's journey can bring great peace into your own life. I found myself riding right along Meredith's side asking "Now what?" No matter where you are on your path of awakening, this book will enlighten you!"

— Nicole Gabriel, Author of *Finding Your Inner Truth* and *Stepping Into Your Becoming*

"Meredith has created a uniquely inspiring roadmap that plops you directly in the driver's seat of your own life and propels you forward with amazing tools to send you to wherever your heart desires. Her stories and experiences expose you to an amazing world few see or are aware of and gets you in touch with just how powerful you really are. Hold on tight because your journey is about to begin. Enjoy your ride!"

— Patrick Snow, Publishing Coach and International Best-Selling Author of *Creating your Own Destiny*

Jen—
Believe in your
power and intention.
Dream Big, Hold on Tight
& keep your heart open
wide.

BECOMING
RIDICULOUSLY
AWESOME

WHO
DOESN'T
WANT
THAT?

MEREDITH HERRENBRUCK

AVIVA
PUBLISHING
New York

Published by:
Aviva Publishing
Lake Placid, NY
(518) 523-1320
www.AvivaPubs.com

Meredith Herrenbruck
Telephone: 415.999.7675
Email: Meredith@ROIexperience.com
www.ROIexperience.com

ISBN: 978-1-943164-98-1
Library of Congress: 2016958147

Editor: Tyler Tichelaar
Cover Designer: Nicole Gabriel/Angel Dog Productions
Interior Book Layout: Nicole Gabriel/Angel Dog Productions

Every attempt has been made to source properly all quotes.
Printed in the United States of America
First Edition

Ego says, "Once everything falls into place, I'll feel peace."
Spirit says, "Find your peace, and then everything will fall into place."

— Marianne Williamson

DEDICATION

I dedicate this book to all those who have trusted deeply in themselves enough to have fought and pushed through their self-imagined limits to get to the other side, even though they may not have known what the other side was yet. It takes courage and a leap of faith to believe that somehow it will all work out. Thank you for your courage—it allowed me to find mine.

To my father, Elbert Bressie: You inspire me every day with your wisdom and strength of will. You showed me how to shine my light in all the dark crevices so that I no longer needed to be afraid. You allowed me to feel safe and okay with my premonitions and to explore my gifts and share them with others. I am grateful for all you have taught me, for the world you have shown me, and for believing in me.

To my mother, Leslie Bressie: Thank you for being my teacher in all the ways you have. Your sacrifices are noticed, and I am grateful for them.

To my husband, Marc Herrenbruck: You shine my mirror brightly back to me so that I may become ever more awesome for myself, for you, and for our family. Without you, I would not laugh as much. You make me laugh every single day, and for that, among so many other things, I am grateful. Thank you for your support and love and sense of adventure. You are truly my soul mate, with whom I am so glad to share my life.

To my daughter, Elyse: I saw you before you were born, an image that flashed before my eyes, and I knew you would take your father and I on a journey of great love, dedication, and delight. You are growing and learning in such amazing ways—I hope you grow fully into yourself and that your cup overflows always.

To all my teachers: Everyone with whom I come into contact, brush past, or even share a smile with, you are my teacher. Thank you for the lessons; thank you for your wisdom. If I don't get the lesson yet, I am sure I will soon—when the time is right.

ACKNOWLEDGMENTS

An enormous sense of gratitude to the following who have inspired me along my journey through this life:

Sai Baba, Dannion Brinkley, Paul Bressie, David Bressie, Denyse Browne, Albert Einstein, Buckminster Fuller, Deborah Jones, Luis Kahn, Gay Luce, Robert Monroe, Jed McKenna, Michael Mulligan, Maharaj Nisargadatta, David Patten, Baba Harihar Ramji, Manu Saito, Marvin Shagam, Sobonfu Somé, Mrs. Terwilliger, Brian L. Weiss, M.D., Hank Wesselman, Ph.D., and Lisa Winston.

CONTENT

INTRODUCTION

AN INVITATION TO SEEKERS

If you have picked up this book, you may already be aware that your life is seriously stuck somehow, yet there is still a possibility of your life getting better in some way. Everything might be perfect except that one thing that you know would make your life more awesome. If you can't think of what that thing might be, ask yourself, "What hurts the most?" Do you feel that your current relationships are frustrating and perhaps near an end? Have your family members driven you so nuts since you were little that they trigger all the right things in you to make you stay away? Do you wish you could actually like the job you have or could even get the job of your dreams, but it just doesn't happen? Somehow, you are miserable in some way where you are and perhaps in just the ways you are. Something in your life stays stuck, and you just can't shift it, no matter what you have attempted. You try and try to make things better, but somehow, it stays the same, so you can't make any progress.

But what if you finally could make it better, and what if doing so wasn't as hard as you previously thought? What if you didn't have to suffer and take your lumps? What if you didn't have to suck it up and make do with what you have? Well, you have heard of the Law of Attraction, right? What if I told you that you are telling the universe exactly what you want, but that all the things you want are pointing in all different directions, or in ways you are not yet aware of? When you are aiming in so many directions or the wrong directions, then you can't go anywhere. That, my friend, is exactly what keeps you stuck.

If only we had a solution to change those signals, right? I was extremely stuck, too, for many years, and I tried to overcome a host of issues, including to overcome depression from a childhood trauma, frustration with not feeling heard, having a hard time connecting with people the way I wanted, not being majorly triggered by my family, and generally feeling out of place with the world. I feel your pain because I have lived through similar pain. I went to therapists and sat there at one point spinning my wheels, just talking for talking's sake and not moving forward anymore. I needed lasting solutions that propelled me beyond my current state. What did I do? I found new tools! And once I started to understand *how* I was stuck and that my old thinking could be overridden for the better quite easily, the sadness and frustration started to go away. The new and better choices and belief systems about myself and the world were now overriding the old and outdated. I started being able to look and move forward toward greater success in more and more parts of my life. Know this: No matter where you are, it can be better. You just need to apply the right tools. Once you do, you can let go of the past and see your life get easier and so much happier. No matter what your religion or spiritual beliefs, these tools are not designed or intended to interfere

INTRODUCTION

with that, but to complement your life in all the right ways.

In this book, I will help you unblock what stops you from moving forward in life and achieving the success you always wanted. I will share with you stories that will inspire you to know that you are not alone in your pain and that people can have more success than they imagined. I will teach you how to get unstuck from recurring patterns, triggers, and even nightmares. I will show you that you have all the resources you need to take your next steps in the direction you want.

This book is divided into three parts to help guide you through major areas of your human experience. The physical and mental aspects of our world are our first stop. They expose the tip of the iceberg where we most notice the effects of our unwanted experiences. Good news! This is also where you begin learning how to make lasting positive changes and shifts. The second part addresses how to incorporate these tools into your life and how the more you feel whole and complete, the less you will need to rely solely on *out there.* The final part introduces you to wonderful healing practices that will expand your awareness into some other influences of your life you may not be aware of, but should. Throughout the book, I guide you through exercises and easy-to-use tools to ground you, empower you, and make you unstoppable.

If you apply the lessons in this book, then there is almost nothing you can't achieve. You can have better connection and more meaningful relationships. You can feel more fulfilled at work and create your dream job. You can be more balanced in yourself in more situations at home and with family and friends. And if you keep applying these techniques to all parts of your life, then you can become ridiculously awesome: full of balance, happiness, joy, and abundance.

I know all this is possible for you because I have already taken the journey. I grew up in Northern California as the youngest of three kids and the only girl. Ever since I was little, I had premonitions of events in my life or my family's lives months in advance of them happening, and in trying to find the answers for why and how I had them, my life has become quite a journey. I received my architecture degree at Cal Poly in San Luis Obispo and for many years renovated homes. My father's interest in the "woo-woo" led me to Nine Gates Mystery School in 2000 and to neuro-linguistic programming (NLP), where I am now a Master Practitioner and Family Soul Constellations Facilitator. I later studied with a Kahuna in Hawaii and got initiated above where the Hawaiian goddess Pele breathes her magic on Kona. Through these experiences, my intuition has only been enhanced, and now I am proud to say I am a Kahuna, a seer of that which is unseen. Our family ranch in Montana taught me that not only am I part of everything, but how important it is to listen: to horses, plants, all things because everything has its wisdom. I now want to share with you the aha moments I experienced on my path and the amazing tools I've discovered. Today, my husband, our daughter, and I live in San Anselmo, California with our Vizsla dog Tucker, our Jack Russell Terrier Sprite, and two chickens, Lola and Penelope. Consequently, I see clients in Marin County, California, but also often over the phone or Skype. The wonderful thing about this work is that even if a client is on the other side of the world, this change work can take place just as effectively.

You too can have equally ridiculously awesome experiences and find greater excitement about your future. But I know why you haven't started. You are overwhelmed; you don't know *where* to start. Part of you is going one way, and another part is going another. It's hard to look at something new when you are busy being overwhelmed and overloaded with the past. I bet you feel that nothing has worked so far, so why start something new and be disappointed *again*? You are busy with your world, don't have time, and you have been to so many therapists who all say the same thing…and nothing changes. Think of this, though. Your past doesn't equal your future, does it? No! You can't drive your car forward while looking in the rearview mirror. Instead, let's drive forward together into your future of awesomeness.

Please let me help you. Let me be your mentor, coach, and your greatest advocate. I am passionate in what I do because I know what I have learned works. I want others to experience the breakthroughs and aha moments that I have. I will show you what stops you and how to move through your obstacles. I will show you the many layers that create your experience and how to manage them, clear them, and soon have more ease and success because you did so. I know you want to get the most out of your life and just want more normality and more abundance, more ease and more access to the resources you didn't know you already had. I have enjoyed witnessing many clients experience great surprise at their profound results and the speed at which they find aha moments. They have experienced lasting change and success with the tools and resources I offer. You want that too, don't you?

So, are you ready to take that little leap of faith with me, to try something new and improved from your old stuck habits and pain? Don't you want to have relief from the past so you can focus more on your amazing future? You've heard it before: Be the change you want to see in the world…and other similar things. I am here to tell you that is possible. I even have the solutions to help you figure out the signals you are sending so you can learn how to shift them to become more aligned and go in *one* positive direction only. Once you feel aligned, not only will it be easier on your brain, emotions, and spirit, but you might even sleep better and have more fulfilling relationships, too! After a short time...the universe will hear you and say, "Yes," to whatever you would like and deliver it on a silver platter. Now...what would you like?

Let's begin, shall we, to see how exactly you can get it, and how you can Become...Ridiculously...Awesome.

Meredith Herrenbruck

"The significant problems we have cannot be solved
at the same level of thinking with which we created them."

— Albert Einstein

AUTHOR'S NOTES

To protect the confidentiality of my clients, I have changed the names and sexes of people mentioned in stories in this book.

Please notice the symbols and descriptions on the left page of each chapter. I have chosen each one to correspond with its accompanying chapter's information to help create a little more insight for you. Symbols are actually quite interesting and apparently more than just an image or a representation for whatever they symbolize. Symbols are everywhere and have been used for millennia. That's because they can be quite powerful. They hold energy according to their users and carry a depth of meanings. Not only are there symbols for math, religion, and direction, but also for healing. Consider this—if people use a symbol consistently and with focus, does that not make the symbol in itself more potent?

When I was at Nine Gates Mystery School in meditation years ago, I actually saw some of these symbols and drew them in my journal. I had never seen them before, but when I asked the staff about them, they explained what they were. At the time, I thought they couldn't possibly have real power, but I have since learned that I know far less than I thought. I am constantly being shown more about the universe and its many hidden treasures—so I continue to accept experiences as I receive them.

A colleague of mine shared with me how to get even more information from symbols. You can understand a lot of their meaning if you imagine that symbol in your pineal gland (mind's eye). Like a 3-D holograph, you might notice the multitude of layers of information stored in these symbols. Enjoy!

PART ONE

THE PHYSICAL

SNAPPING OUT OF YOUR OLD
PATTERNS TO FIND RELIEF

Raidho: A rune that means wagon or chariot. It also means travel, in physical terms or lifestyle direction, also, seeing a larger perspective and deciding on the right move for you. Runes were used among the Germanic people from the first or second century CE. The root word Run- means secret or whisper.

CHAPTER 1

MOVING BEYOND SURVIVING

"It is not the strongest of the species that survives,
nor the most intelligent that survives. It is the one
that is the most adaptable to change."

— Charles Darwin

Becoming ridiculously awesome is a wonderful pursuit, isn't it, so why wouldn't you want to experience that? When you do, you feel expansive, bright, amazing, inspired, and well, awesome! The feeling moves far beyond those of drudgery, sadness, blahness, sickness, frustration, or lack of motivation. Just step into that feeling of stuck-ness for a quick moment and then pop out of that experience. Come back into your seat here and now and at neutral. Think of pink elephants dancing on the roof in polka dot boots. Are you back now? Smiling a bit? Good.

Now, imagine yourself as a big, bright diamond glistening in the most amazing sunlight. Ah, that's better. The diamonds are strong, yes? Brilliant? Clear? And it took time, just the right resources, and a lot of pressure for them to get that way, right? Similarly, as your life has pressure and stress, you become the most amazing diamond the world has ever seen—in just the way you are. I will help you get yourself through and beyond that pressure—the caked-on dirty part (I'm sure you have had enough of that in your life)—and get you more into the brilliant clarity part where the light shines through and makes your soul truly sparkle.

Some of the greatest people I can think of had extremely challenging moments, worked through them, became more powerful, and exceled in their lives! For example, Mark Wahlberg dropped out of school at the age of fourteen, and two years later ended up in jail. Years later, he became a famous musician, actor, and producer. Oprah overcame sexual abuse, racism, and sexism in her life and work. She is aligned. She is purposeful. She radiates her truth. I can show you how you can do that, too. So, if you are tired of holding all that stuck-ness together, constellated in your emotions, body, and spirit, it's time now to let it go. Let's grab your polishing cloth and start polishing. Let's rub off the caked-on dirt, leaving it in the past appropriately, with thanks and forgiveness, where it belongs, and polish you up. Let's bring in more awesome, please!

Over time, as you let things go and polish away the tarnish, your life will become easier. I would like to add here that *becoming* ridiculously awesome and *being* ridiculously awesome are not the same thing. After the conscious and mindful work has been completed, you are left with a state of being where you are more consciously and fully present here, now. The more awesome you are, the more often you are, and the more you consciously choose to be, the less you will be fighting the elements and the more you will be appreciating your experiencing. You live it, breathe it, you are it, because there is simply nothing else to be. Only then does that state of being become your default state. You leave the past behind and become fully present— just you, being ridiculously awesome. How cool is that?

I invite you to use this book—all of it. Write in the margins; highlight key phrases that resonate or inspire you. You bought the whole book, so make it work for you. After you read it through once, re-read it to fine new and deeper meaning. All that you read may not click with you at the same time. You might even hate some parts. If that happens, it's actually a good thing. Ask yourself, "What irked me about that? Why do I disagree?" It might lead you to good, meaty stuck-ness. Most importantly, be patient with your process and with your evolution, too! It will happen in just the right way. It always does. Think of it this way: If you eat a meal (or take in too much information, for that matter) too quickly, you get a stomach ache (or your head blows up!) and you reject what you just digested. No fun. But if you are patient and open to this process, your soul will be nurtured in beautiful ways, and you will be more open to letting things go. You will already be growing and expanding into a happier place. That's what your goal is, isn't it?

Louis Kahn, the famous twentieth century architect, would hold a brick in his hand, studying its unique characteristics, and then ask students who were stuck on a design, "What does the brick want to be?" A brick is perfect for creating arches and being in compression. It does not, however, have qualities suitable for making a tension bridge over a gorge. Steel is more suited for that, as the best engineers have discovered. Just like people, every material has its own unique qualities and strengths. It's up to us to listen and create an environment that allows those qualities to be expressed in the best possible way. Connect with your wisdom, see your uniqueness, and stop trying to be like everyone or anyone else. It's a pointless pursuit. I have tried that approach and found it did not get me where I thought it would. It didn't fit, and it didn't do me or anybody else any good. I know you are being the best *you* that you can possibly be. I'm here to help you do *you* even better.

Renovating homes and the process of helping clients draw a lot of parallels for me. I am enthralled to look beyond the surface and try to bring forth the inherent character of a space and let it shine out into the world. If I am working on a craftsman home, I'm not going to try to make it Rococo. If it's a log house, I'm not going to try to make it feel Mediterranean. That wouldn't make sense, would it? No one would feel comfortable with it in the end anyway. The energies, styles, and sensibilities get all confused and the space wouldn't know what *it* was. Nothing would be aligned nor singing a single, poignant, beautiful tune. It would be a complete mess!

For you and your journey, it's important to carve out space to notice what is already whispering to you. What do you already know? What have you always wanted to be or do but were always stopped from doing in some way? If you can't quite think of it yet, let me tell you a little about my own home and the joys of renovating. Maybe it will highlight for you something you may want to shift or create, even if it's something as little as wanting to organize your shoes by the door—something that *just keeps not happening*...for some unknown, wacky reason.

MOVING BEYOND SURVIVING

Completely covered with thick layers of ivy sitting as high as your hip, this garden had seen better days. The ivy was choking other plants and hiding yellow jackets, broken pots, and even a Radio Flyer we would later discover. The shingles on the house were stained and cracked with age, and the rooms hadn't been updated in a long while, but this 1908 craftsman home we were hoping to buy had charm, an earthy elegance. It had character. My whole body vibrated while looking around this place. I buzzed around in delight while investigating and making plans in my head. I was listening, too, to hear what it desired to be. My husband and I saw beyond the clutter, the hoarding of the current owners, painted shut windows, the piles of clothes, boxes, and things stuck in every nook and cranny. We imagined beyond the existing old, ugly carpets and a bathroom that just reeked of mold. (We quickly shut *that* door and moved on!) Very few people would be able to see past all the neglect and tiredness, but I could. I was born to it. This place was a diamond in the rough; the tall ceilings, two (ahem) "working" fireplaces, and big windows were just some of the features that told us the house could be amazing. A deep front porch with a teak swing begged us to enjoy it. I just knew this was our place. I *felt* it. My husband shared the excitement, yet deferred to me to make sure it could truly become something awesome. Growing up in a home that was constantly being renovated, I have been tweaking my surroundings ever since—always eager to fix anything up and make the experience better for both the building and its inhabitants. No problem, we agreed. It will take six months. Ha!

I graduated from California Polytechnic State University, San Luis Obispo (Cal Poly, SLO)—one of the top five architecture schools in the country, and it was extremely competitive. It required long hours enduring physics, surviving calculus, crunching numbers over three pages of engineering calculations (my dyslexia made this quite a challenge), burnt fingers from hot glue guns, going through too many X-Acto blades, one trip to the ER, not much sleep, and a lot of digging inside myself to create a masterpiece in white foam-core.

These projects got personal—very personal. As a student, you and your project breathed as one. And when it came time to critique, where your teacher and peers would criticize and challenge your model, it felt like they were ripping both your final precious design and you to shreds. Many students on the receiving end of these critiques ended up feeling very small and shattered. Some even ran crying from the room. It felt like a cruel form of punishment, to be opened, exposed, and criticized in such a way. It was rough, and you often questioned your sanity for choosing such a demanding major/profession. You put your *soul* into these things, spending weeks on and even bleeding for it, quite literally!

I learned a very important lesson in third year design when my teacher said—while the class stared at the floor, some in tears, and all of us battling our emotions after a heavy afternoon of critiques—"*You are not your project.*"

Now, let that soak in for a minute. You are not your project. Kerplunk! That weighty stone of wisdom sank deeply into my soul and landed, sending ripples throughout my awareness. It is such a completely obvious statement, but it was profound for me. There it sat for all to witness, that pearl of wisdom I wished would have been shared a long time ago—like on the first day of the first year of college. But we are experiential beings; we honestly learn best by doing and aren't ready for the next lesson until we are ready.

My brain contemplated this new idea, poking at it for loopholes. First came the excitement, which quickly turned into denial. *How is that possible?* I thought. My ego was front and center, ready for battle. Objections came out of the woodwork. This new information quite possibly could dismantle all that I had done and felt I *was defined by* up to this point. Ouch! But this was architecture, so sometimes you have to start over armed only with the wisdom of previous failures.

> "There is no such thing as a failed test.
> You will learn every time you challenge yourself."
>
> — Marsha Blackburn

Once I got past the denial, the good news/bad news negotiation started. Then, after going over all possible alternatives and being satisfied with the new proposition, came acceptance. I might as well try something new since the last experience had completely wreaked havoc in so many ways. I had worked through all of the objections, and upon finding fewer and fewer, and eventually finding none, I thought, "Yes, this is a better idea and makes much more sense." My system relaxed and became more at peace. I had found a new equilibrium.

Then came the relief. I didn't have to stick to the old pattern of self-doubt any more. Elation erupted. What freedom! There was so much pain and frustration, fear of not measuring up to others' standards, and sleepless nights before. But really, to what purpose had I gone through all this—to end up in anguish and feeling twisted? So I chose the better option, replacing old beliefs and frustrations. My ego lessened its hold as the advice from this trusted teacher sank in further. What's more, after the transition in my mind and soul, I felt power. Not the dominating kind of power, but the power of expansion, confidence, ease, and calm. And it felt *really* good. The truth was the truth. Why argue with that?

I explain this experience in such detail because it is important to understand the multi-dimensional choice-making process we go through all day long—with each choice being made in a nanosecond. If you are stuck in a behavior or belief, try pulling that single moment apart. You might be able to see all that occurred in making that choice. It wasn't just a yes or no answer, but it was comprised of multiple consultations with various parts of yourself that needed to weigh in on the matter. That single choice was actually made by a huge summit meeting.

I finally waded into applying this new perspective more and more throughout my classes. Since my beliefs had changed, my behaviors naturally shifted as well. I felt more at ease distancing myself from my creations, and I was more objective about receiving criticism. As time went on, my projects resided emotionally outside of me more and more and successful experiences added up. My perspective on the whole critique scenario shifted on its weary little head. Critiques weren't meant to tear you down—quite the opposite, in fact. They were solely analyzing the project to shed light on how the project *aligned* with its forms, space, structure, and design. My classmates and teachers were sharing wisdom on how to go deeper and more thoroughly develop ideas to create one cohesive, amazingly-experiential, and visual piece of architecture.

When I stopped resisting the lesson and feeling the need to protect myself, my world elevated. I saw things differently and was able to experience things I previously could not experience. The final result of this whole process was that I was naturally able to allow myself to be at this new level, without thinking about it. When my thinking changed, so did my actions. Polishing. Polishing. Polishing. So how do you get your life into greater cohesion and aligned to directing yourself where you want to go and what you want to be?

Exercise

Sit comfortably and close your eyes. Imagine popping out of yourself and looking back at the you that is sitting over *there*. What do you see? Are you a fixed, constellated program of outside input, or is your experience dynamic and multi-faceted? Can you now experience and know that you are the catalyst in your own life? Note your experience.

_____

_____

_____

_____

_____

_____

_____

_____

_____

_____

_____

_____

The Trauma

I carried a lot of baggage with me into college, and like everyone else, I was still figuring *me* out. But nightmares had plagued me since high school. A novel I read roused my memories of being molested as a child, and I would wake up screaming with tears running down my face. Not only was the memory infiltrating my daily life, but the perpetrator remained physically in close proximity. He was an employee who often worked in our home, and my father refused to fire him, until years later for theft. Until then, I felt trapped and didn't know how to make the situation better. I became angry every time I saw him, and I would yell at him, but never about the truth. Imagining the repercussions scared me silent. Between living my life, learning how to master architecture and college, figuring out how to be a contributing person in the world, dealing with my demons, and looking for answers, validation, and a whole host of other things, my plate was full. This experience from long ago and far away filtered through everything. I just didn't know it yet, but I was in the center of a storm of my own making.

Depression was constant, but awareness of that occurred only many years later. When something is your norm from childhood, you don't know any differently until things start to get better. Only from a new perspective do you notice the structure of how things were. I thought my experience and everyday sense of being in the world was normal. Always a bit withdrawn, mistrustful of any kindness people would show, I would second guess and rebuke any generosity. Trusting anyone to a deep degree, despite his or her amazing kindness, was nearly impossible. Although it was lonely, I did a good job being alone because, well, I felt it was safer. It seemed like the best idea I could come up with at the time, but it was an unfortunate side effect to my choices.

Experience/Belief Loop

Life is a series of aha moments, and then it plateaus while we learn how to implement our newfound perspectives. First, we don't believe the new truth/wisdom; we can't imagine it is so easy, and then we have to spend time slowly applying it to our lives and making sure it really works. See, we humans operate in a very specific way. Our brains are hardwired to survive things, which is good, because if they weren't, we probably wouldn't be here in the ways that we are. We have to survive the environment—not only the weather and other animals, but other people—and learn to operate in society. Sticking together promised a greater chance of survival, so it was mutually beneficial to make nice with others and help each other out.

The thing is, once we have had success with a particular behavior, thought, or feeling—we have been rewarded in one way or another—we file it away as having worked. The synapses get formed between thought, action, result, and belief and remain connected until they get broken by a better offer, and new synapses are created for that better offer. Until then, we unconsciously create a filter that blankets everything in order to keep having similar successes. Our brains, those meaning-making machines, file those positive experiences away and attach beliefs and meaning to them to be applied when needed. What you experience, you believe, and what you believe, you end up creating and calling a success.

Better Offers

As time passed in college, I started to have new experiences and was exposed to more fun. I kept surviving these new experiences, so my critter brain (or Reptilian Brain; the part that runs the basics of our survival: fight, freeze, flight, food, fornication) had to adjust its thinking and thus began to settle into this new pattern. My world opened up to so many new friends, and my system had to accept that compassion, fun, and an enjoyable college social life really did exist. When the happier moments started to clash with the old sad feelings, something had to give. With all these experiences, my system was getting an update it sorely needed.

I also started to believe that if my life could be better in certain areas, it could be better in other areas, too. Despite the fact that my social life was improving and confidence in my craft was increasing, I also realized there was no controlling my perpetrator, or what anyone else was doing or not doing. I could control myself, though. Somehow, everything I thought and felt started and ended with me. But I didn't know where to go or what to do to move—in any direction. I was trying to get over it, but I didn't know how. I was seriously stuck. So out of desperation, I started looking for pearls of wisdom. I didn't know much, but I did know that those pearls got me to better places, and that was exactly where I chose to go. Sometimes, things just have to get bad enough that you will finally reach out for something better.

Inch by tiny inch, moment by tiny moment, I grabbed on to such pearls of wisdom as, "You aren't your project," and things started to shift and get a bit brighter. If that project wasn't me, and if I could be objective about foam core and ideas that came into my head, maybe, just maybe, I could be a little objective about my world and the me in it. Rather than being tossed about in my own storm, what might be possible if I were outside of it looking in? And if I were outside of it, maybe I could even make changes. *Maybe I had a choice.* Just having that thought changed the foundation of my whole world.

> "The keenest sorrow is to recognize ourselves
> as the sole cause of all our adversities."
>
> — Sophocles

Another part of this experience also warrants sharing. Ever since I can remember, I have had premonitions. They haven't happened that often, but they have tended to be about more important events in my life and my family's lives. First, they would come in dreams months in advance, and later, they would come a few days in advance. I would see something happen in real time, and I was powerless to stop or change it in any way. In high school, it got kicked into high gear, too, so there were many times I didn't know what reality I was in: the dream-state of the future or the here and now. This experience made me question exactly how the world worked. So many questions were invoked. It also helped me start to trust that life would work out because I saw that it already had. If I were able to see the small windows into the future, then certainly there *was* a future, and I was there in one piece and doing okay. That bit of knowledge got me through more fearful moments than I could count. If the future, which hadn't happened yet, were true and real and couldn't be changed (as far as I could tell, and I tried!), then I had to *trust.* I just had to put one foot in front of the other and know it was going to work out.

To get even further along, I needed to start trusting those around me. I had to let people in. Mrs. Terwilliger was the highlight of my fifth grade field trip to the sea. She was a lively old soul with a straw hat and a twinkle in her eye. She would dash about in the forest and on the beach, singing, "Gather around children! Something special!" and she would show you the marvels of a sea star, an urchin, or a small shell. She even taught us how to make a little volcano on the beach using a mound of sand with a long stick in the middle running from bottom to top. She put in a little tissue and lit it up. Amazingly smoke came out of the top. It was a simple trick, yet very delightful. Her tone held such wonderment and authority in everything she described that I was captured by her enthusiasm. She lit up my childhood and made the world a special place. Her energy radiated kindness. She was a beautiful soul, through and through, with no ulterior motive. She was one of those people who made you believe that not all people are bad. And if one person I came across was that way, then perhaps there were others, too. My family, and the Bay Area, for that matter, all still remember Ms. Terwilliger, and though I knew her only for a few short hours, her essence permeates through my life.

Do you have someone like that, who can take you out of your own perceptions and add magic to your life? We all need someone like that. Those pearls can be found in people and also in experiences. You might be surprised if you look back to see how many you have experienced. Be open to more of them, and let them go when they need to move on. Life is not about clinging but enjoying as you can and letting people and experiences go when the time is right.

Exercise

Write down who adds great delight to your life and acknowledges you for who you are. Who can you trust and lean on to help you when times get tough (even if you only see him or her rarely or for just a moment)?

arielle, annush, Thomas, Mom, Dad, julie

As I kept trudging along my path, I started looking for these pearls in my life, these moments of iridescence and resonance. And once I found those pearls, certain parts of my life got brighter, easier, and helped to balance the other parts that were still in bad shape. Perhaps the *looking* got me to find them more easily. And how did I know that moment, that path, that right choice was a pearl? It took a long time to figure out how to identify these qualities. I had to compare and contrast them to others I had found when possible new pearls came along. I did have a sense that the quality of a given event, thing, or person was different and unique, and my gut would kind of say, "This is it. Follow it." Because it felt brighter, it felt more solid. My whole being vibrated as a harmonic; it was amplified. I now call it "following the ribbon of light," but back then, I was just picking up the pieces and seeing where they took me. Surely, making that choice had to be better than where I was.

listen to your gut, follow the ribbon of light

At least this theory was a start, and something I could work with. It took me many years to figure out that I only have myself to control. And if I were going to do that, I had better learn how to do it in a way that would make me happier—I really, *really* wanted that. Have you ever been there, in that loop, hoping to get out but not knowing how—all the while trying to live your life the best you can and have things move forward like you think they should?

When the Student Is Ready

When I was in doubt about life working out, my father would say to me, "When the student is ready, the teacher will appear." That Buddhist Proverb makes me laugh now because it's really how life works, don't you think? You are ready when you are ready, and then the universe will give you the next puzzle piece to work out. It might be odd to think of the universe being a co-creator of your experience, but haven't you noticed that once you learn a particular lesson through and through, it stops presenting itself to you? Do you think it's an accident? It's magnificent! It's because there is no need to go through it anymore. Whenever you keep facing a particular challenge, ask: "What is it there to teach me?" or even, "Why do I keep wanting it in my life? What good thing comes to me when it's there?" I will flush this out in more detail later, but once you get through a challenge, you will have leveled up. Your perspective, energy, and attention have shifted, and you align with the world differently. You are simply radiating a different vibration, and the world will simply respond in kind. If you take the literal meaning of universe—one song—it means that everything down to each atom is all working in perfect harmony. Once you learn more about how this greater system works (keep reading!) and work with it, not against it, you will be even more empowered and able to choose more consciously the life you want for yourself. The more objective you can be about your choices and experiences during this process, the easier it will be to make leaps and to shift things into better alignment to get yourself where you want to go.

"Big results require big ambitions."

— Heraclitus

46

What Would You Like?

Why would you want to look from the outside in anyway? Well, you don't unless you want to shift something so you are able to go somewhere or get something, right? In other words, you want to have a certain experience that you may not yet be having. And if you want to make something better, you need to figure out what you want. What would you like? It seems like a simple enough question, but for many, it may be the first time someone has truly asked you and truly wanted to know the answer. Your life may have had many hardships, and you may have been raised to react, get out of the way, and just make ends meet. Or you already feel you have tons going for you, yet there are some areas that you want to enrich.

What would you like? Not something someone else has to change or something for *others* to do. You can't control other people at all. And I would bet we have *all* tried to do that! But you can always shift, evolve, and change your thoughts, beliefs, and actions. Those are not as fixed as you might have previously thought. You can always choose how you would like to experience your world and what you do in it. If you can imagine the experience of feeling, thinking, and doing what you desire in the future, you can then figure out the bridge, all the necessary steps to making the change happen. Every great journey starts with a great first step—figuring out what you would like. You have to know where you are before you can figure out where you are going. We do it when traveling to unknown lands, so why not do it in our personal lives? And it's okay to ask for what you want. Seriously, it's okay. You have to give yourself per-mission right now. Once you have done that, then let's get on with it. We have awesomeness to achieve!

The importance of *how* you phrase your goal is equal to the desire of your goal itself. Let's look at some details that will help.

Make it an internal action. As I said before, you can't change other people. Not your parents, spouse, coworker, none of them. Getting mad at them and being disappointed in them doesn't help. To quote Dr. Phil, "How's that working for you?" What works more effectively is to shift your feelings about that person, relationship, or behavior so you can be more balanced and at ease. What do you want to experience in yourself?

Keep it positive! Why? Our subconscious always says yes to anything it experiences. If someone says to you, "Don't look down." Then you look down. "Don't touch the stove." You touch the stove. The amazing thing about our brains is that we always take the subject of a sentence and say yes to it, even if the operative word is "don't." It's more useful to say, "Look straight ahead at that tree"—then the person is more likely to do so. If you are leading others in a meeting, instead of saying, "Stop chatting," say, "To get on with our day, let's go through the next three items on the list. Sarah, what do you have for the first item?" You have to lead your brain to where you truly want it to focus and stay put. Energy flows where attention goes.

Make it attainable! If you ask for something too big, then it will be hard to get, or take longer to get, or even be outside the realm of your belief system, and that might discourage you from making it happen. Instead, make it just the right scope for you to know you have it. You can always add the next steps later as a new goal once the first is complete. But know that your thoughts, feelings, and actions can successfully align together. The more aligned you are, the easier it is to achieve your goals. To put icing on the cake, be specific. Now that we have learned how we are wired and what makes us stuck, let's uncover how we make the better offer to our system.

Exercise

Write down five things you would like more of in your life, or five things you would like to shift or make better. Make sure they are things you can and want to change within yourself. Keep the phrasing positive!

For example:

Not so great answer: "I don't want to be poor." Where is the focus? Being poor. Don't you want to put your focus on something else more fulfilling?

Better answer, but needs tweaking: "I want to have a million dollars." There is a positive goal and you are looking into the future.

Better yet: "I want to be more open and energized about creating my financial success for the next five years."

1. _____

2. _____

3. _____

4. _____

5. _____

Dagaz (day or dawn). A rune meaning breakthrough, awakening, awareness, transformation. The power of change is directed by your own will.

CHAPTER 2

MAKING THE BETTER OFFER

"What would you attempt to do if you knew you could not fail?"

— Dr. Robert Schuller

The first step in renovating our home was to make a plan, to see past the existing, and look to what could be. The vision we had was put into play with drawings, planning, and executing it all with the contractor. Our design never wavered and only improved with some evolving eyes and ideas as the project progressed. I will admit we were ambitious on the timing and thought it would all be easy. It was only going to take six months, of course. Well, it ended up taking over a year and a half. There were tons of surprises, but we kept our eye on the prize—a beautiful home that would support our lives and be the backdrop of our daughters' many memories.

We knew some parts of the house had been neglected, but when we opened the walls, we were shocked to see rat nests in the upper floors and walls, and rotten studs you could pull apart by hand in the master shower. Not good, but it was what it was. Were we just going to cover up the rats' nests again and hope they didn't exist? No way. Surprises kept coming, and we went on a roller coaster of emotions, but even so, the foundation was strong, the floor plan was amazing and gracious, the location perfect, the grounds with mature trees were fantastic. We just had to stick with it and trust the process—and trust our team and each other. We had to know that it would all work out. So we kept moving, past the peeling away of the layers and the surprises, and stayed focused on the inevitable result that would come with our persistence and vision.

I want to assure you that you have that perfect foundation. No, it may not be like anybody else's. That's actually a great thing, if you think about it. You are unique and amazing, and you got here today in your unique way, so you are ready for the next step! Yes, you might clear some dry rot away. Yes, you may want to get rid of all you don't like (and you can in good time), but remember your goals before you get your sledgehammer out and go swinging—otherwise, you might take down a load-bearing wall. Slow and steady wins the race, and you have many years yet to enjoy your life here on earth. Let's get to the root of your strengths and resources and build from there. Remember what you wrote in the last chapter—what you would like. Please review it now before reading further.

Welcome back! Now that you are fully present here, let's continue. Doesn't it seem weird to think about what you would like and not what you don't want? Typically, we are so used to being in a certain state that we can only move on to another when we have a picture of what we want. Think of being at a restaurant looking at the menu. Do you look at what you want first off? Or do you first eliminate what you don't want so you can make your final choice? What if there is something on the menu you have never heard of? Do you choose it, ask about it, or avoid it all together? Maybe it just sounds too scary. But what if the server explains how wonderfully tasty it is, telling you it is the best thing on the menu? When your server explains all the reasons you would enjoy the dish, it's easy to make that choice. And then you say, "Sure, why not?" When you take your first bite, relief floods your system because it is something you relate to. Though it's a bit different, it is close enough to your comfort zone to make you feel safe taking that leap so you keep eating.

We will make those leaps (or shifts if that word feels better for you) if it feels safe enough and if it fits with our image of ourselves and our world. As you already know, our systems are amazingly and smartly designed to want to stay within the parameters of what is safe, because it's a known entity—it already works. We will choose to leap when we feel safe in the new location/experience/feeling, when the threatening, "It won't work out and is potentially fatal," is minimal, non-existent, or gets us what we want. We filter through so much information throughout the day and our lifetimes. We are constantly scanning and saying, "Yes, that's me," "No, that's not me," "Yes, I like that," "No, I don't like that," "Yes, that's safe," "Hell, no, I am *not* doing that!" We are filtering, filtering, filtering, all the time, checking new information against old, comparing and contrasting, and then making the most appropriate choice we can to stay alive, safe, and happy.

Consciously Filtering

When you ask yourself, "What would I like?" you are setting a forward motion in your mind. You are swinging an arm forward, imagining what

53

could be, and taking the idea for a test drive. When you allow possibility, you are actually creating space for it to enter into your life. You are setting up your internal filters to notice this new thing when it truly does come along. You are setting yourself up as an amazing net for opportunity!

To begin being more conscious of your filters, keep asking yourself, "What would I like?" Do this again and again, in happy times and sad, despite any potential obstacle. Do it especially during the sad times. Do it even if people may disapprove of your new choices, even if you expect a zig and there is a zag. This is your compass to go by...*all the time*. Never stray. Like in *Moby Dick*, your eye is on the prize: the white whale. Yes, I know that in that book Captain Ahab dies after being obsessed with capturing the whale, so you may think this is a horrible example to use, but I recently heard a new perspective on this whole book that I would like to share with you. Jed McKenna, who wrote *Spiritually Incorrect Enlightenment*, came to the conclusion that on the surface *Moby Dick* seems like a tragic tale, but from his perspective, it's a book about enlightenment because he recognized that we go through the same transformational process when we move into enlightenment as described in the book. The novel is full of many religious references and a lot of challenging dialogue that seem to support his conclusion. Even so, at the end, the men are in the water. One may assume they died! But if everyone died, Jed asks, who then wrote the book? "Call me Ishmael" the story begins. Given this new context for *Moby Dick*, I feel justified in using the white whale as my example. The white whale is the symbol for relentlessly going beyond your own self-created boundaries and breaking free of what others are telling you life should be like. Only you can determine that answer for yourself.

You have to trust your filter, your vision, and live by it. That is easier said than done initially, I know, but it does work. You might have voices in your head steering you in a different direction, but don't listen to them. They may be from the past, just thoughts created to keep you out of potential trouble. Like I learned in the story from the last chapter, "You are not your project," perhaps you are not those voices, either. Let us have them take a backseat until we get some things sorted out, shall we? Trust in yourself and don't get distracted. Stay your course, even if you don't know where it is going exactly. Read on and I will show you how this process gets easier.

Now, this is where we get into the big bad world of the things that stop you from changing and shifting. Our world has a lot of distractions. Your family structure may be keeping you in your current place and role. Doubt may be trickling in. And when doubt and distraction seem to make up your whole world, it's not easy to sift through it all. It is so all-encompassing. It is everywhere you look! But take one step with me, just one! And then another. Stick with it. The more you do, the more you can do with ease. The reinforcement from each success will naturally propel you to leap more often with more security and enthusiasm.

Making Shifts/Leaps

Once your filters are placed in the more conscious arena of your world, you might already see shifts start to happen. Why? Because you are now more actively choosing your world and not being as reactive to it. You might even notice how your *perception* shifts about the past and old triggers and how that frees you from your current stuck-ness. What are you noticing differently about yourself? I have had clients who feel that if they shift, some judgment from somewhere in the world will cause them great harm—not physical, but emotional harm, and that can be just as terrifying. But let me ask you this: Are you worth it? Is your happiness of greater value to you than potential loss? Would you rather be happy from the inside out, spilling your exuberance and natural beauty out into the world where so many more people would benefit and then respond in kind? No one can live your life but you. No one faces the mirror, looks into your eyes, and knows all that you are, all you are capable of being and achieving. You do, though! You do, and it's up to you to live your life how you see fit. And if you believe it, so will other people. Keep your wheels turning and you will get traction!

Whenever you feel life getting too hard, please be reminded of Frederick Douglass, a black slave born in 1818, who created for himself a remarkable life despite his many obstacles. Have you ever heard of him? Reading his first autobiography, *My Bondage and My Freedom,* changed my world and made me feel so inspired by his incredible and compelling bravery. As a young slave, he would hop over the fence to the next house to meet Sophia Auld, who taught him to read. Despite the very real threat that he would be whipped or even worse, he chose to learn to read. According to *The Norton Anthology of American Literature,* "Douglass understood even as a young child that whatever his white owners wanted him not to have was certainly the most valuable thing for him to seek...." He took his world and challenged it, and you know what? He ended up years later becoming a social activist, journalist, prolific speechmaker, and ambassador. If he could do it, then I could certainly get some more bravery and challenge myself—and level up a bit. How could Douglass excel where few could? The obstacles he faced were so severe. What did he believe that made his actions possible?

Exercise

Who inspires you to be brave and do what you feel is right for you? In what ways?

_____

_____

_____

_____

_____

_____

Imagine stepping into that person's experience and gathering all the great beliefs he or she has. Breathe it into all your body parts to see whether it gives you any insight. What comes up for you? What do you experience? What are you thinking and feeling?

_____

_____

_____

_____

_____

_____

Exposure and Experience: Doing What Works

When we are born, our brains are developed enough to connect with all the body parts needed to live and make living happen every moment of every day. You don't have to think consciously about breathing or beating your heart or looking toward a sound. It's all automatic. Our critter brain is fully operational, handling the instincts of fight, flight, freeze, food, and fornicate. It takes care of our survival. Gross motor skills are part of the package, and life experiences help shape our thoughts, feelings, and actions. Seeking pleasure is already loaded in the brain's software, but we all have our unique ways of doing it. We are shaped by our experiences—our failures and successes.

The brain—your fabulous brain!—is designed to learn in a way that facilitates the best possible chance for survival. It wouldn't make sense if it didn't. We, as a society, wouldn't progress very far if we were not programmed to survive. If some action or way of thinking works, then it gets happily filed away, to be used in the future when needed. Part of this evolution is that whenever we are in a state of fear or anxiety, our body releases adrenaline (epinephrine) and other hormones and neurotransmitters. In these moments, our brain looks for the quickest way to find safety. For a salesperson, it's to not pick up the phone and call. For the house painter, perhaps it's to avoid the ladder or climb down as fast as possible.

When an infant is hungry, it cries, hoping for a positive outcome: getting fed. The parent picks the infant up and goes through the list of needs the infant usually cries about, right? The parent is looking for success, too, to get the child to stop crying. Once parents know their children are hungry, they immediately feed them and the infant brain synapses connect the response (getting fed) to the action (crying)! If the infant could think, its thoughts would be, *If I cry, I get picked up and fed. Great! From now on I will cry and I will get relief. This works!* Stress is relieved and happiness floods the body. Synapses are created. *I think I will do it next time.* Synapses are reinforced. Over and over, this will happen in a million different ways as the child grows. When there is a need, the brain will light up and send a signal to the part of the brain that has already stored the successful experience (in this case getting food), and then the child acts in the same way to be successful. It worked last time, right? And on and on it will go throughout life. The child learns what works, throwing out what doesn't.

Success!

I am sure you are thinking that this is obvious, and perhaps it is, but how about when we apply that same logic to how the child experiences the world emotionally? What happens when the child's physical needs are not met, which in turn means emotional needs are also not met? I read an article about Ugandan children in an orphanage who don't cry because there are so many children to care for, it is impossible to see to all their needs. So the children adapt. They solve the problem: They don't cry. They have found crying to be useless, without purpose. Their immediate needs didn't get met, so they adjusted their belief structure and their actions.

We little beings are sponges, soaking in all we see, hear, sense, touch, and experience. By the age of two, 80 percent of our beliefs about ourselves and the world have been set. By the age of two! This means that anything new that comes into our realm is judged by the experiences we had before we turned two. That's all we can do, right? We choose the best we can using the resources we have at the time, and we will keep using the same information until something better comes along. By the time life happens, skipping along at its own pace, our beliefs

59

are firmly entrenched and it's hard to shift gears. When was the last time you had a summit meeting inside yourself to help you understand why all your parts were doing what they were doing? Exactly. We don't operate that way until we get really, really stuck on something big, where our current situation does not match up with our skill set (that is based on a survival skill we created when we were little). How very annoying!

If we get rewarded for behaving a particular way, then we choose to keep behaving that way. But what happens when the outside world stops giving the reward that we know and love? The pattern has been set in stone, so what are the options? We either adjust our beliefs (which are experienced as solid truths) or stay stuck, and we wonder why things aren't working out the way we want them to. Usually we muscle our way through each frustrating situation to try to make the existing paradigm work. This is exhausting and rarely fruitful. We end up imagining that the world is against us. We buy rabbits feet to change our luck. We wish on a penny and throw it in the fountain. We go to workshops only to come back feeling the same and thinking we wasted our money. We sink into the feeling that "This is my lot in life. Nothing can change." But it can, and you have all the resources you need to make a change. Let me share with you an example.

A Little Phobia

Here is a question for you: Do you have a phobia or some little fearful habit you can't get over? I had a terrible fear of spiders. Ugh. The fear of spiders was paramount and I freaked out whenever I saw one, even if it was smaller than the head of a pen cap. My body would get all squirmy and I would get as far away as possible. I would muscle through my fear and take it outside on a piece of paper or in a cup, but I was uncomfortable all the way—worried it would somehow run really fast up my arm and into my nose or something.

Ever the supportive man, my dad tried to help me out of my predicament. He said to me, "To get over your fear, you have to learn more about spiders. *Knowledge* will get you over the fear." My dad is perfectly wise, as all dads are, so I heeded his advice. "I will endeavor to learn all about the spider," I thought! National Geographic programs would come up and I would force all the cells in my body to sit in that chair and learn about the beauty of the spider, its amazing web creation, its fine hunting skills, its procreation…. And the longer I sat in that chair, eyes glued to the television, the more my skin would crawl—the more my brain was saying, "You are going to die!" I would even watch *Arachnophobia* over and over, trying to fix my problem. I was a glutton for punishment, I guess, but I stayed, because my dad was not wrong in my eyes. What he said made sense, right?

Sigh. Are you laughing yet? Yes, I thought you might. A few things are happening in this story:

1. I had a horrible fear of spiders.

2. I went to my dad for help and he shared his wisdom with me. I tried his wisdom, and because he could never be wrong in my eyes (because you never want to think your parents might not be absolutely correct about everything—that would rock your world, sending you tumbling into scary places), I stayed and watched each spider show to the end. And yet?

61

3. I was still deathly afraid of spiders.

4. Surprise! Nothing changed. Every time I saw a spider, my brain would kick into high fight or flight gear. What was going on?

Why did I not get over my overblown fear? After all, it's a spider, not Godzilla. I didn't understand until I finally discovered one teensy-weensy detail I had overlooked in this whole scenario; I didn't want to make my mom wrong, either. Let me explain.

Upon delving into my past in a Neuro-Linguistic Programming (NLP) practice session, my memory bank found that my mom was deathly afraid of spiders. Apparently, I had witnessed an incident when I was about five years old where my mom was screeching at my father to kill the spider in the corner of their bedroom ceiling. I was watching this and learning, soaking up all the experiences, as any child does. In this case, I was learning from my mother what to do with spiders. Not just what to do, but how to *feel* about them. Feelings are part of our survival toolset. And wanting to keep a close connection with her, I chose to do what she did, and so I did what any child might do. I would choose to fear spiders, too. And that was the Intended Positive Outcome (IPO)—to be loved by my mom. The unintended positive outcome (UPO) was to be afraid of spiders. Well, that's just fantastic!

> "When you have fear then the world is a big place.
> When you have courage then the world shrinks."
>
> — Stephen Richards, *Releasing You from Fear*

The Imprint/Root Cause

There I was, in quite a pickle, and in quite a state of angst about what to do and feel about spiders. (Your phobia might be different. It might be a person, a conversation with someone.... It's not about the subject, it's about how our choices get implanted right under our noses without us even thinking about them. It happens so quickly!) So, back in NLP class, we had uncovered the whole map of who, what, where, when, and why, and thus got an appropriate update to the system. By disconnecting the synapses from stimulus to the response, and then making new connections that were better offers to my brain and psyche, I was able to change my experience. And now, I can look at all spiders without fear and can put them outside with more ease and calm. I'm not saying that I will be having a tarantula as a pet anytime soon, but my system is much more neutral about them—though still aptly aware when a dangerous spider should be avoided. That trigger was cleared. What a relief that now I don't have to have that fear tie me in knots anymore. Success!

A colleague recently shared with me his story of a client who had years of therapy to get over her fear of chickens. Not only did the elimination therapy and other therapies she tried not work, but she was poorer by over $17,000! Yet, in less than an hour of working with my colleague, she was cured. I want to impress upon you that if you are not experiencing results in your current therapy, and it seems that the therapist is only too happy to see you for years and years, it's time to challenge it and make a change for something that works.

Obviously Elusive, Elusively Obvious

When a long pattern of behavior and thoughts have been with us since we were little, we don't think it's anything but normal, right? Right before our very eyes, like a second skin, our existing patterns and behaviors become our fixed reality. They color our world and shape and influence our experiences. Because it has been that way for so long, we don't even think to look at those things. They have become part of us and permeate throughout.

If we are so used to the norm, it's hard to reach for something better. Why? Because it has already been implanted that we have found the best solution to the problem. What fires together, wires together, and it remains that way until the better offer comes along. Old synapses get unlinked and new ones connect up when those new choices get made. Although some of those rules or solutions may have become constellated in our worlds, our brains *are* constantly evolving, learning, and shifting, so rest assured that things can change and get better. As we are presented with lots of choices, we filter out some because we can't comprehend them. We keep filtering until we find what suits us.

Yes, we learn math, physics, English, and increasingly more complex thoughts in school and life, but what we don't do consciously is apply them to how we feel about ourselves. Men, in general, are taught to toughen up, don't cry, and be a man (whatever that really means) from many generations back. Women were taught to be quiet, learn how to care for a family, and to multi-task. So many outside forces, such as our families, spiritual or religious advisors, and communities reinforce our behavior because we are taught that it worked then, so it should work now, and if you don't like it, you are plumb out of luck for making it without our support. So our choices are based on this:

64

MAKING THE BETTER OFFER

If something gets us the two things we want most in the world—to be safe and to be loved—then that's what we will do.

Being safe and loved—that's what it's all about, baby.

"Our stresses, anxieties, pains, and problems arise because we do not see the world, others, or even ourselves as worthy of love."

— Prem Prakash, *The Yoga of Spiritual Devotion*

Society, since its beginning, has been all about staying safe. We bonded together to get out of sticky situations. We needed each other for heat, health, acquiring food, and keeping ourselves safe from predators—saber tooth tigers, bears, snakes, spiders, and more. We relied on each other's skills, and we shared a fire around which stories would be told. Many of those stories would be fantastic and epic—and they would often weave in wisdom, as learned by our forefathers and foremothers, to keep us safe. As society evolved, social norms and rules developed that all could understand and abide by. Roles were understood and lived by in our families and in society as a whole. And more often than not, our role became attached to our identities.

Notice, now, the smaller society: the family unit. This is where we are raised and cared for in all the ways we are, for better or worse. Children learn what works and what doesn't work in that microcosm based on those who run that unit. In *Love's Hidden Symmetry: What Makes Love Work in Relationships*, Bert Hellinger says, "In the service of belonging, conscience reacts to everything that enhances or endangers our bonding. Our conscience is clear when we act so that our continued belonging to our group is assured, and we have a guilty conscience when we deviate from the norms of our group and must fear that our right to belong is jeopardized or damaged." Some situations offer greater resources and some not as much. If your safety net was threatened by what you did or didn't do, thought or didn't think, believed or didn't believe, you either had to drop your beliefs to stay in the good graces of those around you to make life happier and more tolerable, or you had to maintain your beliefs and go it alone.

As we get older and begin to understand the family structure better, since we have survived up to this point, the brain is happy sticking to the status quo. It works according to how it gets rewarded. When peace, safety, and security are attached to certain choices, the critter brain sees *success*! It then thinks, *I survived and thus I am happy. I will keep doing what I have found to be most successful.* When a choice is seen as less successful, that information gets stored, too, in the: *what not to do* files. As pleasure-seeking creatures, we always move to where we think the greener grass is.

But then outside influences encroach on the family unit. We attend school with other children and teachers who have different experiences and life lessons. We engage in conversations, learn about different cultures, read the newspaper; whatever the new source of information is, we are getting more input. We have to decide how to receive it and what to do with it. And even though many think the new information is a good thing, it often challenges the successful systems we have created for ourselves. We learn, we grow, and then sometimes, we just get stuck when there is a conflict between the old input and the new. The new input is in discord with the older, existing input. We can choose either to adapt the old or to embrace the new.

MAKING THE BETTER OFFER

It's always a choice that comes down to us.

The reason people often don't change is any new choice has to go up against what is known and feels safe. Will my parents be angry? Will they withdraw their love? Will they withdraw financially? Multiple norms are being challenged. Those filters are on overdrive. All those challenges are pointing to the age-old root question: *Is this survivable?*

Out of love and loyalty, we often want to stay within the family system to be safe and loved, making choices accordingly. And if we move outside of these norms, then we take a leap and see how it works out. If it works out well, it gets uploaded as something to do again. If not, then adjustments are made until the system gets the proper rewards and it's back to normal and happy.

We cannot learn to make better choices. Why? Because we are already always making the best choice we can. But we can learn to put much better items on our life's menu.

> "It's not the chooser who's got the limitation.
> It's whoever makes up the menus."
>
> — Carl Buchheit

Why It's So Hard to Change When You Want To

Let's apply the question of why it's so hard to change to everyday life. Here's what happens. You start with situation normal. Life is happening as it always has. You have your friends, family, job, home, car, dog, certain clothing style, etc. That's what you know and what you are used to doing and being. All is good. All the reinforcers of your world—the people, places, things, belief systems, society, and family that are part of your identity—are in place. When you change something in your life, sometimes it sets off warning bells in your head. The challenge arises— if you change, what will happen to your relationship with those outside reinforcers? Maybe nothing negative, only positive results! But your system is constantly scanning for the best survival choice and has to check the potential choice against all that is already safe and survivable.

If you imagine our growth and life like that of a chambered nautilus, you will notice that it starts very small, in a chamber, and then when it outgrows the old, it makes a new chamber slightly bigger than the last, but still quite similar. Our beliefs about ourselves and the world slowly expand as we grow and expand outward into the world. Our worlds still seem the same, but over time, subtle changes are made. These moments of expansion or transformation are a direct result of our ever-shifting belief systems. When we are comfortable enough to feel that the choices we make will not be a threat to our survival, to our being loved and belonging, and this new thing is something we desire more strongly than we fear it, we expand our world by trying this new thing.

Give Yourself a Pat on the Back

I want to take a moment to back up, take a breath with you, and get a bird's-eye view. If you think that up to this point you haven't gotten life right, then you haven't given yourself enough credit. Of the millions of decisions you have made, and continue to make, you are always making the best choices for yourself. In every instance. With the information, energy, feelings, and situation you have, why would you choose something *not right* for you? Think back on a time when you didn't act in your own best interest. There may have been a time or two when you didn't really make a decision, feeling the choice didn't matter much one way or the other, and it would work out, whatever you did. But I would be surprised if you ever actively chose to totally screw yourself over. Now step into this feeling of accomplishment, this knowing that you always make the best choice. Then breathe it all in and step into the youngest version of yourself—breathe with those little lungs and wiggle those little toes and fingers—and tell your tiny self that he will always make the best decision. What a feat! When you are ready, grow that little one up with that new knowledge until you get here and now, sitting in your seat.

You have made the best choices you could with the resources you had, so why are you still beating yourself up? Acknowledge and feel empowered by the fact that you are already doing the best you can. Know that the next choice might be better for you. If the choices are not getting you where you want to go, and someone else is benefitting from those choices, ask yourself: What good comes to me when I choose that? There is a reason—deep down, there always is. Look deeper and be honest with yourself. Honesty with yourself will get you far, and it will clear out those cobwebs of uncertainty and fear.

You gain strength, courage, and confidence with every experience in which you really stop to look fear in the face. Like Eleanor Roosevelt, you are able to say to yourself, "I lived through this horror. I can take the next thing that comes along."

What Might You Lose of Value?

Because our choices are all internal, we subject them to many rules of our own making. It's not as simple as: Make a choice and be happy. If it were that easy, you probably wouldn't be reading this book.

Reread what you wrote in the last exercise. Imagine what you would like, and step into that experience. Imagine yourself in the near future already having what you want. Imagine it and step into that experience. What good things do you notice? And what negative things or objections do you experience? Take a few moments to close your eyes and focus on this.

Great…now step out of that experience and feel yourself in your body now. Set yourself to neutral.

Exercise

Write down any objections you have experienced. Secret: Your objections are what stop you from getting what you want.

_____
_____
_____
_____
_____
_____

So if you come across a behavior or pattern that no longer works for you and you really want to change it, you have to figure out what stops you from doing so. You need to tease apart those elements and make a better offer to your system—only then can you shift into a new pattern and behavior. Your system says, "Yes, it's survivable and pleasant even. There are no objections at all anymore. I'm okay with that. Wow, that experience is *much* better than what I have been going through."

As you choose to shift consciously through action and habit, there will be a subtle identity shift. Others in your life might not like the change. Why? Because it challenges *their* identity and *their* choices. As Jed McKenna wrote in *Spiritual Enlightenment: The Damnedest Thing,* "People do not like their reality fucked with."

> "You will never find the real truth among people that are insecure or have egos to protect. Truth over time becomes either guarded or twisted as their perspective changes; it changes with the seasons of their shame, love, hope, or pride."
>
> — Shannon L. Alder

Failure/Making Mistakes

I want to talk about the concept of failure. I'm sure part of you is perhaps uncomfortable with shifting in any way because it might set off fireworks in yourself or your family system—or work or somewhere else. Failure gets a bad rap, I believe. The word has so many negative connotations, and society as a whole gets really down on failing. We have to succeed! We cannot fail! We end up stressing out to the nth degree because of this great fear. Let's ask this important question from a 1,000-foot perspective looking down on someone who has "failed." That person tried something and it didn't work. Okay. It didn't work. Now what? That person files it away and uses that experience to propel herself forward, right? The only real failure would be if nothing was learned and anguish and mental spinning occurred. Thomas Edison failed. Nikola Tesla failed. Steve Jobs failed. *Everyone* has failed. Abraham Lincoln failed. The only difference is that they were able to use the knowledge of what didn't work to find what *did*.

J.K. Rowling recently spoke about failure. I am sure you know of her resounding success with the Harry Potter books. At the lowest point in her life, her fears and her parents' fears "had come to pass." But in that time, she learned something amazing about failure, which propelled her into great success.

The benefit of failure, she said, is "the stripping away of the unessential. I stopped pretending that I was anything other than what I was and began to direct all my energy to finishing the only work that mattered to me. Had I really succeeded in anything else, I might never have found the determination to succeed in the one arena where I believed I truly belonged. I was set free."

How does this apply to you? You have to jump—with both feet, eyes forward, heart happy, and ready for what comes next. You have to trust that life could be a little better in a month, a week, or even in the next moment. You have to be okay with your life, for a moment or two, being messy while you rearrange your world. You have to be okay with your family and friends perhaps not liking you poking and prodding and moving walls—tearing down barriers to yourself and others. You have to be okay with the roof shaking and your world getting a little dusty. You have to be okay with the possibility of them surprising you and *loving* the change. You may not always know what they are thinking and believing. To find out, I find that an honest conversation with those you love and fear losing is a great way to sort things out. It might be scary, but isn't it better to know than to assume something which is false? You might also grow closer from the experience. Remember, you have a solid foundation!

"And once the storm is over, you won't remember how you made it through, how you managed to survive. You won't even be sure, in fact, whether the storm is really over. But one thing is certain. When you come out of the storm, you won't be the same person who walked in. That's what this storm's all about."

— Haruki Murakami

For many years, I feared my parents would reject me if I confronted them about the sexual abuse I had endured and for not ever firing the guy until many years later. From high school on into my twenties, I had varying conversations with my mother about the incident, so I know they were informed by the housekeeper, whom I told the day it happened. It was said that they never left me alone with him from that point on. But in those conversations, I was still not getting what I wanted or needed emotionally. I thus remained stuck. There was a key piece of healing here that I needed my parents. Once I had that realization, my psychologist suggested I write my parents a letter. I typed it up, but I was so incredibly fearful of their response that it sat on my desk for months, just waiting. I literally shook in fear at the thought of that conversation, of all the possible repercussions, and the fear that somehow I would not get the acknowledgment I so desperately needed. It got to the point where I felt I needed to push through my pent up fears and just do it. I was tired of being in that state, and moving forward finally seemed like the better option. I was exhausted from living in fear. It was time to move past this—there was no cheating the process. I just had to do it. For my healing, I needed to clear out my energy and share my feelings and experience—and to give them credit, too, for being able to be open and responsive. They were adults and could take care of themselves. I hoped they would appreciate where I was coming from, and if they didn't, then I just had to live with it. We all have to walk our own path, stand in our own truth, and let the chips fall where they may. Trusting that it would work out was a very tenuous idea at that time, but that polishing cloth needed to come out.

The whole thing was kind of like a story Karen Salmansohn tells in her book, *How to Be Happy Dammit,* about a criminal facing punishment by the king. The king offered two options: a secret punishment hidden behind a big scary iron door, or the noose. The criminal chose the noose, but asked the king before his death:

> "So, what's behind the door? I mean, obviously, I won't tell anyone," he said, pointing to the noose around his neck. The king paused then answered, "Freedom, but it seems most people are so afraid of the unknown that they immediately take the rope."

Self-Limiting Beliefs

A client, Leyla, was frustrated at her husband because he wouldn't help clear out the garage for a car that she wanted to buy. Because they only had one car, she felt very limited. I asked her why she didn't buy the car and park it on the street until the garage was cleaned. It might give a visible incentive to her husband. "Well, no!" she said. "Cars get so ugly and dirty when they are parked on the street."

"What if it's only for a few weeks, and then you get it washed before you park it in the garage?" I suggested.

"I suppose that's okay. But what about all the stuff in the garage? I can't just put it in his office on the floor. I'm not that type of person! That's rude!"

"If you make an agreement with him on a timeline, and then the timeline wasn't met, perhaps a solution could be found that works for you." She pondered this until I said, "I know that when you want something, you go for it, finding a way to make it happen; you find the how because your desire is strong enough to carry you through." Then I asked, "Where would you go once you had your car?"

She paused for a long time before admitting, "I have no idea." As you may realize, not knowing was the real reason why the garage was never cleaned out in the first place and why she had not yet bought a car.

The Invisible Umbrella

Our belief system is created so quickly and perfected so early we don't even know it has happened. As time passes, that invisible layer of belief blankets our future and our whole experience to such a degree that we are no longer aware it exists. Our belief system is not experienced as beliefs, but as steadfast rules. Like the Law of Gravity, our beliefs are there, they function in a certain way, and they are unchanging. When I asked Leyla if she could simply get her car washed, making her belief system an offer that she felt okay with, she ended up taking it.

When we peek in to see how a belief system was created and how it is structured, we can then find what is necessary to challenge it so we can make the better offer. We have to be willing to challenge our pre-conceived notions to expand our world again, to look at things in a new light. Once those new possibilities become available, taking the steps to where you want to go is that much more likely and achievable. If you don't have your goals clearly in mind, then the rest of the world will *seemingly* be preventing you from getting what you want. We are always the true culprits in sabotaging (and creating!) our own future.

The main trick in life—and how to become ridiculously awesome is: Be honest with yourself during this whole process. To get past the *suffering* part that has occupied your whole experience up to this point, you have to clear out what no longer serves you. As a result, more and more parts of you will naturally align to your goals because what previously stopped you is no longer there. When all parts are going in the same direction consistently, how could you not be achieving your goals? Impossible! Now that we have already started letting go of what we might lose of value, let's reinforce our experience by acknowledging a few but very important rights.

"Your beliefs become your thoughts,
Your thoughts become your words,
Your words become your actions,
Your actions become your habits,
Your habits become your values,
Your values become your destiny."

— Mahatma Gandhi

Exercise

When you imagine what you would like, and you have stepped into that experience, ask yourself, "How will I know when I have it?" What will you be thinking, feeling, and doing when you already have what you would like? How is that different from where you are now?

_____

_____

_____

_____

_____

_____

The Mayan symbol Hunab Ku is likened to the yin-yang symbol. It represents the bridging of opposites, connecting one's inner being with one's external body. Achieving oneness with the universe.

CHAPTER 3
LEARNING YOUR RIGHTS

"A house must be built on solid foundations if it is to last.
The same principle applies to man; otherwise, he too will
sink back into the soft ground and become
swallowed up by the world of illusion."

— Sai Baba

Now you know why we choose our survival skills, what stops us from changing, and how we can motivate ourselves properly to start moving us in the direction we want. Let's start getting to the point where we can start updating our software programs and having a better experience; gently leaving the past pains behind with ease and grace and getting some new skills (improving on old ones!) to apply on that subconscious level, rather than muscling through everything all the time and being exhausted and overwhelmed. You know the definition of insanity, don't you? Doing the same thing over and over and expecting different results. Let's try something new and different, shall we?

Give Your Parents a Break

Before leaping forward, we have to look backward sometimes, and looking at our parents is our first stop. From generation to generation, we all make the best of our circumstances using the resources available to us, taking each experience moment by moment. Try as they might, parents cannot be perfect for their children or create a perfect experience for them—things can and do get bungled up for so many reasons. The perfect message gets lost in delivery—lack of sleep, stress, our own triggers come up to bite us in the behind…. Yet parents are always doing the best they can.

Let's play the devil's advocate here to drive this point home. Do you really think any person is actively trying to do his worst, to make everything around him horrible and unlivable? If he were, that would mean he was doing his best to be his "worst." He would still be doing his best, even though the outcome, on the surface, appears to be his worst. When we apply this idea to guiding infants while we are sleep-deprived, stressed, overwhelmed, and learning how to care for a baby—and trying to figure our own selves out—there is bound to be a translation error. So even though there are generations upon generations of parents doing the best they can, trying to make life better for the next generation, it will still never be perfect because you also have the decision-making of the child who makes her own decisions and adds her own beliefs. Kids will create some magical thinking, too, to make their experiences palatable.

And often, kids will blame themselves for their parents or caregivers' behaviors. Think about this question: Would your parents have acted any differently if you had a perfect stunt double in your place, who looked and sounded exactly like you, but wasn't you? Probably not, because they are already operating on the imprints and patterns that were installed in them when they were little. Parents may not intend for things to happen as they do, but they work with the circumstances, doing the best they can—and here we are. Yikes!

The child sees and experiences all she does; then makes her own decisions about what has occurred and lives life accordingly. Why? To be safe and happy. From all the decisions that have been filtered through her brain and filed away accordingly, she selects the best survival options and, hopefully, thrives in the world. What does the child need to grow and prosper most successfully? Rather than imagining a million things to filter through, be relieved to know that it really comes down to five basic needs, with each need building on the success of the one before. Dr. Wilhelm Reich, born in 1897, was an Austrian psychoanalyst who understood human success was predicated on these five needs. These needs are called the Reichian or Organismic Rights. Between the ages of zero and two years old, these needs get imprinted at successive times with the last two stages being imprinted during the same time period.

Our Organismic Rights

1. The right to exist (0-2 months)

2. The right to need (2-6 months)

3. The right to be assertive (6-12 months)

4. The right to be independent (12-24 months)

5. The right to love and be loved (12-24 months)

When that development during that particular window gets misinterpreted, interrupted, disturbed, and/or traumatized, however, the child will tend to default to certain sorts of behaviors and belief systems to compensate. Tension may be held in certain places in her body (which later can turn into illness or pain), or triggers and sensitivities to certain stimulus may occur, all in an effort to survive and somehow make her existing world okay and "normal." The consequence is that what you survive, you recreate for future events, no matter how seemingly small and insignificant the imprint.

Let me give you an example of how this might occur. If a child between the ages of two and six months experienced a conversation between the parents or even a feeling from a situation that results in, "I just can't afford anything any more emotionally or physically now that we have kids. I'm maxed out." That child, picking up on the anger, words, and energy might make a decision at that point to try to survive the best she can given the environment and make a choice about how she acts and what she believes. Perhaps if we stretched out that moment of decision-making that little one has, it might go something like this: *I will act in ways that I don't need. My needing stresses out my parent(s) and I don't want that. I notice that when they stress, they get mad and it scares me. I don't think I can survive that if that happens.*

I read a great summary of this work at nlp-practitioners.com: "When we are challenged, encouraged, informed, and supported through these stages, we expand and are biologically, emotionally, and cognitively ready and available for the opportunities, challenges, and changes of each succeeding stage." The more successful the input is at the earlier stages, the more successful the resulting beliefs and actions of the child will be for the future.

LEARNING YOUR RIGHTS

All these developmental stages of these rights occur before the age of two. So the old, dismissive adage "They're just kids" should be thrown out with the trash. These gentle, bright beings absorb everything, making decisions to set the course for their best possible outcome. At nlp-practitioners.com, it also says, "When we are less than fully successful at navigating through a stage, the results get stored in our bodies as 'body armoring' and the energy stuck in the pattern and the un-evolved parts of us are not fully available for the next stage." When the flow of love and energy gets interrupted, then the beliefs and actions result as follows:

1. If I don't exist, I won't bother them.

2. If I don't need, I can just be loyal and giving.

3. If I'm not allowed to be assertive, I will not assert myself.

4. If I don't have the right to be independent, I will rely solely on others.

5. If I can't love and be loved, I will not connect and be isolated.

"Negative emotions like loneliness, envy,
and guilt have an important role to play in
a happy life; they're big, flashing signs that
something needs to change."

— Gretchen Rubin

Exercise

Write down what things you didn't like experiencing as a child that still hurt—things you would like to be better or different. Perhaps you didn't get enough positive attention from a parent or enough time with someone. Perhaps you really wanted to be acknowledged for something, but you didn't get the feedback you felt you needed. If you go through the needs above, what makes you more emotional than the others?

_____

_____

_____

_____

_____

In *The 5 Love Languages: The Secret to Love That Lasts*, Gary Chapman describes the five love languages to be:

1. Words of Affirmation

2. Receiving Gifts

3. Acts of Service

4. Quality Time

5. Physical Touch

Using examples of various couples, Chapman illustrates how these specific behaviors are needed for a healthy relationship. When these needs were met, the couple was happy. So if one person loves getting encouraging words more than the other needs on the list, and the other person only gives the other four, there will be frustration. Aha! My brain started to tickle in memory as I was reading Chapman's book. A theory developed in my mind that this particular frustration is one of the compensatory behaviors we exhibit when our rights get interrupted. These behavioral and emotional signs can help uncover more of our inner workings and define the belief systems that were installed in us long ago.

To break it down in direct terms, it seems that Words of Affirmation correspond to our right to exist. Receiving Gifts corresponds to the right to need. Quality Time corresponds to the needs of being separate and yourself. Acts of Service correspond to the right to be assertive and take action. Physical Touch corresponds appropriately to love and being loved sexually. It makes sense that our behavior is driven by our interrupted needs and our attempts to correct this. I love giving gifts, and my husband loves words of affirmation. After I read Chapman's book, I found out how helpful it was to know my husband's language and use it appropriately. I now write little notes and stick them around in surprise places, and I say meaningful words of appreciation to him more often—and he *loves* it! Why not use what works to bring you closer together in understanding and love?

I think using these Love Languages benefits relationships wonderfully, but I feel it's also important to read through them and check into which language you are most drawn to or resonate with the most. It might lead you to notice where you are still stuck or hurt. Let this insight be a guide, but not a complete solution for all the challenges in your relationship. Overall, the more we are open, clear, and in proper balance with our significant others, the more fulfilled both of us in a relationship can be because we are more available.

Acknowledge, Acknowledge, Acknowledge

While we are opening ourselves to acknowledging our stuck feelings or frustrations, it is equally important to acknowledge our inner child, even when it hurts. If feelings well up, bursting to come to the surface, you are on the right track! You are getting somewhere. Stay with it and know that the pain will not be there forever. Once worked through properly and completely, that pain will be set to neutral so you can move forward to more ease and happiness. Most importantly, in the healing process, it's vital to acknowledge what you have gone through, experienced, and become. Otherwise, you are rejecting all those parts of you that have worked so elegantly to get you here today, in just the right ways.

Imagine you are five years old again. Feel deeply the stuck emotions and experiences where your needs were not met. Tread carefully and with all the compassion you can muster for that little one. Listen to the needs that pop up. Give space and time to that little one so he or she can experience and process through the feelings—but don't feel you need to act. If emotions rise up out of the blue, put them aside. If you are late for an appointment, forget about it for the moment, if you can. Be here now. Help guide that little one in seeing that maybe there are more choices in how to feel and what to do, rather than imagining there is only one option. That is where stress lives! And the more breathing room, compassion, and attention you can give that little one, the more you are, coincidentally, giving those same things to yourself right here, right now. It's the same you!

Try applying this process when you come into contact with others. If tension exists in the conversation, notice whether your ego is in balance. Ask: What does this person need? When you look past all the bluster, you see a little child who didn't get his needs met long ago and far away. Once the need is met and the tension released, the conversation can continue more positively. If you are the one being triggered, feeling frustrated, and yelling, what needs are not being met for you?

That trigger you notice is only an echo of the original imprint where the lesson was installed. Think of a situation where you are overly sensitive and raw and, therefore, easily triggered. Pay attention because it is pointing to you, shouting out, and saying, "Hey! Over here! This hurts!" Then rather than making it everyone else's fault, go inward and acknowledge it in all the right ways.

Exercise

Imagine a young version of you that needs acknowledgment. When did you experience not getting enough acknowledgment in the past? Create a list below of everything you think that little one needs to hear and experience.

_____

_____

_____

_____

_____

_____

_____

_____

You are finally going to give that experience of being acknowledged, in all the ways that little one needs. Now that you have your list, create a younger version of you somewhere to the left of where you are sitting. Imagine now a string between the center of that little one and the you sitting here reading this. Next, read an acknowledgment from above. When you do, also load up that full sensation of what you just read. Once that feeling has almost peaked, imagine stepping out of the you here and now and into that little one who still needs that experience of being acknowledged. Once there, imagine growing that little one up (quickly, in thirty seconds or less) into the person you are now. Do this a few times until it feels complete. Realize also that without that little one who was making all those amazing choices as he or she did at that time, you wouldn't be here today in all the ways that you are.

Tip

If some wound gets too painful at a given time, breathe in deeply in balance for a minute or two. Focus only on the breath and let everything else fall away, being mindful of moving the air and energy through yourself. If a body part specifically hurts, send the breath there to shift and unlock what needs to shift, move, and release. The parasympathetic nervous reflex is activated the same as if someone were hugging you, and that can be immensely comforting. I don't know about you, but I think everyone can use more hugs. This breathing also helps unlock and move the stuck energy through your system and out of your body. What if you don't have someone to hug? Breathe in and out and down to your toes with ease. The acute pain should pass soon.

On a retreat, we used a particular breathing exercise to clear blocked energy in our bodies. The participants turned off their brains and sank into the experience, releasing a lot of stuck feelings, emotions, and energy through movement, breath, sound, whatever their bodies needed to do in that moment. One woman I worked with had rocks for trapezius muscles. I thought it was bone, but at the end of the session, her muscles felt like muscle. She had admitted to having meditated daily, but she never moved the energy through her whole body and through her arms. So it all just got stuck and stored where her attention left it.

"Holding on to anger is like grasping a hot coal with the intent of throwing it at someone else; you are the one who gets burned."

— Buddha

Stepping into Your Power

"If you think you are too small to make a difference, try sleeping with a mosquito."

— Dalai Lama XIV

It might be surprising to feel the lightness as you drop these heavy weights you have been carrying for so long, but it feels so good. If your shoulders have been heavy and are a little more relieved, give them a stretch, and say, "Thank you for carrying that load for so long!" Check in with your body at times and notice what it is telling you. The physical pain may very well be a direct result of the unresolved burdens you have left to tend to. But Rome wasn't built in a day. If it had been, it would have been so boring—missing the process, the peaks and valleys of discovery, and experiencing the plateaus of completion. That is what life is about! Some might say Rome is still being built. It is constantly evolving, for every moment of inspiration, experience, and conversation in the air influences the next. Likewise, you are constantly evolving and discovering the power and essence of who you truly are. The more you awaken to it, the more powerful you become.

Leave No Part Behind

As we start to heal ourselves, we might realize that our experience is not just experiencing the present but also experiencing the past in the present circumstance. The brain is still firing in places still running the survival sequence. There are still synapses giving us the experience that there is more left to do. Our goal is to get all parts of our self going in the same direction, *in the same time.* When our past parts have healed, then there is no threat from the past, and our critter brains will be calmer and more relaxed. Once that occurs, we can put our energy toward creating the now and the future with nothing stopping us. Now that we are building up ourselves with more empowering beliefs and experiences, let's get more tools in proper action after learning how your body *already* works.

"Everybody is a genius. But if you judge a fish by its ability to climb a tree, it will live its whole life believing that it is stupid."

— Anonymous

Exercise

Describe the most powerful and expansive you have felt, where you were just "here, now." What were you thinking, feeling, doing? What else did you notice about yourself?

_____

_____

_____

_____

_____

_____

Ouroborus—This symbol is of a snake eating its tail. Used throughout history beginning with ancient Egypt, through Gnosticism, Hermeticism, and alchemy. It symbolizes self-reflexivity, introspection, the eternal return, constantly recreating itself, endless creation and destruction, life, and death.

CHAPTER 4

NURTURING YOUR NATURE

"I don't want to be a genius—
I have enough problems just trying to be a man."

— Albert Camus

We have looked at nurture—we are built on family and external influences and make choices for ourselves based on this input to create the best possible outcome for ourselves. But what about the nature part of the debate? What else makes us the *us* we know and love? How would we react if all influences were exactly the same across the world?

My husband and I have had many conversations on the Nature vs. Nurture debate. I always find myself asking this question: Why is the only option for Nature and Nurture to be opposites? Why can't it be a little of both? If we are making a metaphor with ice cream, why can't it be a scoop of chocolate and also a scoop of vanilla? (Or in my case, a scoop of mint chocolate chip and a scoop of dark chocolate?) It's a wonderful combination.

How exactly does nature come into the mix? I think that is still up for debate in lots of minds. Our reactions and mental processes are all chemical, some might say. Your mom's diet, stress levels, and hormones all played their part when you were in utero. Our eating and exercising habits, moods, hormones…all those factors of our human experience throughout our lives…are stored in our bodies, but can our current experiences be influenced by previous generations through our DNA? A BBC news article by James Gallagher entitled, "'Memories' Pass Between Generations," stated, "Experiments showed that a traumatic event could affect the DNA in sperm and alter the brains and behavior of subsequent generations." Mice were trained to fear a smell similar to a cherry blossom. The Emory University School of Medicine team then looked into the DNA of the sperm and noticed the DNA responsible for the sensitivity was made more active. Two generations later, the mice were "extremely sensitive" to the scent and would avoid it, even though they had never personally experienced it. Although we can't go back in time and change our ancestors' DNA to have a better experience now, we can perhaps change our DNA through the power of our mind. Our cells regenerate in such a way that every seven years we essentially have a new body. If you learn to focus your mind in the right ways, what's to say you cannot only influence your thoughts and feelings and actions, but your cells as well?

The Power of Mind Over Matter

No matter where you are in life, however awesome or dismal it may be, you have the power of you. You have the power over your choic-

94

es, thoughts, and feelings. If you can think it, feel it, and imagine *its value* in your life, you are more likely to succeed in making it happen, whatever *it* is. Your brain is a muscle that is being fed and shaped by you through food, exercise, emotions, and your circumstances and experiences. Feed it the best you can, for it influences your body's health and your emotional wellbeing. The small successes from the new patterns you set will come with persistent application. Why? The positive results will reinforce the direction you are going. You are empowered by the fact that what you are doing has already worked. That dynamic feeds on itself!

"No·one can make you feel inferior without your consent."

— Eleanor Roosevelt

Exercise

If you don't quite believe in the power of the mind, pick something that you would like to do every day, but have not quite been able to accomplish. Perhaps it's meditation, working out, or just brushing your teeth at lunchtime. Whatever it is, make sure it is something you don't have a trigger around or the sense that it would include any loss of value for you. We want something clean and simple. Now, like in Chapter 1's final exercise, make sure it is small enough, attainable, and positive. The subconscious always thinks in the positive. Imagine all the good things that will come to you when you do it (your motivation). Do it for a week or two, no matter what, and see what happens! If objections come up in your mind, write them down below and look at them objectively. Can those obstacles be released or attended to?

Write down the objections you notice coming up as you are bringing in this new pattern.

_____

_____

_____

_____

_____

_____

_____

_____

_____

Carve Out Space

When I need to relax and focus, I find meditation really helpful. The power of meditation comes from not clinging to distraction and allowing yourself to become focused on *one* thing. When is the last time you actually just did one thing at one time? To have a coffee without planning your day? To pick a flower and just smell it? To be in the moment and only in that moment with the senses you have, and just experience it? We have programmed ourselves to be so busy that we don't make time for this space. And honestly, we need it! If we want to give our greatest selves to the world, we have to give to ourselves first.

I never used to believe in the concept of giving to yourself first. (I didn't want to be labeled selfish.) But once I had a husband, and a dog, and a house, etc., I couldn't get everything done in a twenty-four-hour day. I was exhausted and always looking forward to sleep or a moment away so I could recharge and get back to me—to still-ness. The issue came to a head when I had my daughter. I gave and gave, but I was losing my center and my strength. And what was I really doing it for? To have the perfect house and the perfect garden and everything ironed and picked up and three perfect meals on the table, with fresh roses in the center, every day. Unrealistic? Oh, yes. When I looked at my favorite movies that show a happy, beautiful family with an incredible home, and perfect flowers, hair, and outfits, I let it sink in that it really took a whole crew to make that happen—not one person. I have heard about this day of reckoning from many other mothers. One day we just stop and allow ourselves to readjust our expectations to meet reality where it is. It was time for that reality check and a resetting of goals. The really useful question was: Where was *I* in the middle of all this illusory perfection? Frankly, I was a wreck, yet at the center of my own storm, again. Dammit!

Polishing. Polishing. Polishing. Determination got me back on track, and I pulled on the resources I knew were available. Since I am an early morning riser, I now get my coffee and then sit on the roof and watch the rising sun. I go to bed early so I can do this. I clear my head, thank those thoughts that come in, let them go, and again focus on just being. Breathing in and out, just not thinking anything. Sometimes, I garden; the action is itself a meditation. The actions of weeding or pruning allow parts of my brain to "do something" while the real me is just experiencing, enjoying, and being fully present, not somewhere else. More consistently, I am feeling much better throughout the day and can give even more energy and focus to who I am with and what I do.

Monkey Mind Keeps Monkeying Around!

If you feel you have to be doing something every moment of the day, I invite you to sit for a moment and analyze why you are creating this experience for yourself. There's that choice thing again! I know you are doing it for a great reason, yes. But if you can tease apart the structure of why that experience is held in place, then perhaps you can begin to let it go. We humans are not designed to work, work, work, work with no sleep, no food, and no fun. Sometimes, the balance has to shift to more work for a while, of course. We have to support ourselves, but when something is tipped into a fear, manic, or obligation state so that there is little room for anything else, we can pause, wondering why and how that situation is being created. We are not victims of circumstance. Most of our world, if not all of it, is self-created. So let's empower ourselves by giving back to ourselves and creating a bit of space. And when we do, and connect with ourselves more, we will find greater access to resources bubbling beneath the surface, just waiting to get out.

"You should sit in meditation for twenty minutes a day.
Unless you're too busy; then you should sit for an hour."

— Zen Saying

Find what you like to do that gives you space, breathing room, where you are not pulled or have expectations put on you (either self-created or otherwise) and where you are not thinking but just being. Do this activity for five minutes. If that's too much and your brain, feelings, and sensations freak out, do it for one minute instead. Set the timer if you need to. Do whatever works and gets your, "I've survived and even liked it," feelings going. And by repeating this practice every day, learning to breath and focus, over time you will be able to stretch out the time you can just focus on your breath or a short phrase (called a mantra). You are training your brain for this new pattern. Once it is established, it will be easier and easier to get into stillness and be in a calm space. Again, the more success you create for yourself, the more success will come.

Exercise

Find a small practice and carve out time to do it all by yourself, without distraction. Do it every day. Perhaps it is playing an instrument, meditating, or walking. Keep your boundaries with the outside world to ensure success. Write down your practice here.

_____

_____

_____

_____

_____

_____

_____

_____

Now that you have calmed yourself and focused a bit more, let's get into more action.

As my dad would often say, "Plan your work, and work your plan." During the recession of 1997, he worked extremely hard to save the business he had built up over a twenty-year span. For months on end, he barely slept and was out the door before six every morning, and he didn't get home often before ten at night or later. Then he would do it all over again the next day. Every day he kept at it, using his wisdom, stick-to-it-iveness, and discipline to keep our family afloat. He watched friends go bankrupt around him, those who seemed impervious to the recession—he just worked more efficiently and diligently. Experiencing that incredible resiliency and depth of character showed me I was made from tough stock. If I wanted something badly enough, I needed to dig deep and make it happen. "When the going gets tough, the tough get going," my dad would also say. Since you now know you *are* tough, let's get going!

Following are some tools to help you be master of your own domain:

1. **Get an Organizer/Daily Planner**. **Use it.** I'm not a fan of the digital ones. There is a kinesthetic aspect that I miss, and it's harder to reference "time" when you can't flip pages for the visual and auditory confirmation that page turning gives. Get a paper planner that works for you, and write down your action items. If you are dyslexic, lower contrasting ink/pages are more legible. Pages showing adjacent months help orient us to time better. Franklin Covey Planners are my favorites. https://franklinplanner.fcorgp.com/store/

2. **Write down your goals.** Before you even start with the day-to-day events and tasks, figure out some long-term goals, and then break them down into shorter-term tasks that will get you to your final goal. If you have issues with finishing tasks, plan a goal for *after* you complete your immediate goal. The "If I finish this, then I get to do this," scenario can be useful here.

3. **Review every morning**. Look at your day and write down your top priorities. Stick to seven or so. If you have too many, you feel overwhelmed and unsuccessful if you haven't crossed them all off your list. If your brain is going at night and you can't seem to shut it off, get out a pen and piece of paper, write down what you are thinking about, and review it the next day. Get it out of your system and onto a piece of paper where you can look at it objectively—later—and do what you need to do with that information, dream, or feeling.

Aligning with Your Circadian Cycle and Rhythms

Rather than fighting the world and trying to make your world work around other people's schedules, start noticing and documenting your moods and energy shifts. When you wake up, how do you feel? Do you often wake up in the middle of the night? If so, at what times? When are you most laser-focused? When are you most fidgety and feeling the need to move? When are you starting to look for the coffee or mental stimulation? Looking into the rise and fall of your energy levels and ability to focus on tasks throughout your day will do wonders in helping you schedule your world. Polishing. Polishing. Polishing. You are learning to do what works for you, but you are still in the process of figuring out all the parts of who you are. Of course, deadlines and conference calls can't shift according to your rhythms, but if you had an option, would you rather analyze complex charts and numbers when you are hazy or when you are in the zone and your brain is raring to go? Even more important than managing your time is managing your energy. Documenting your patterns is a great way to pinpoint how you operate and get more joy and connection out of life.

Below is a chart that might help you to figure out what your body is doing throughout the day so you can plan accordingly. It is a chart I have created based on the organ clock used in Traditional Chinese medicine. Since there are twelve organ systems in the human body and two accessory systems represented, each system has its own special time each day when it is operating optimally and with the most energy. Sometimes, however, an organ may be overly taxed or not operating in this optimal level, and you may even notice it! For instance, if you keep waking up between one and three, notice whether you are feeling any repressed anger or fatigue. If so, perhaps something needs to be rebalanced for your liver. It is a great resource for you to help maximize your body's potential and keep tabs on it if there is something amiss.

"We are what we repeatedly do.
Excellence, therefore, is not an act, but a habit."

— Aristotle

Exercise

For the next three days, write down your activities, moods, energy, and eating patterns from the time you wake up until the time you go to sleep. Go to my website, ROIexperience.com, to print out an easy fill-in chart.

Then review what you have recorded over these three days. What could you change, based on your experience, that would make you more effective, happy, and fully present? Record your answers below.

_____

_____

_____

_____

_____

_____

_____

_____

_____

_____

_____

_____

Ingwaz Rune. (NG, the earth god.) This symbol represents rest time, relief, and no anxiety. You feel able to move in a new direction.

CHAPTER 5

DISCERNING THE DIFFERENCE BETWEEN YOU AND THE TAPES

"A disciplined mind leads to happiness,
and an undisciplined mind leads to suffering."

— Dalai Lama XIV, *The Art of Happiness*

Do you remember the story of "The Princess and the Pea" by Hans Christian Andersen? Let's refresh our memories of this little tale. The princess was unable to sleep at night while lying on top of twenty mattresses and even more beds on top of those because that one single pea beneath all of them prevented her from sleeping well. She was successfully labeled a princess for all her sensitivity, and that is where the story ends, which is unfortunate, because she will forever remain sensitive and particular about her set of circumstances. Oh, how difficult life can be if we each only have one magical set of circumstances that will suit us every single moment for our entire life. I think we are made of sterner stuff and don't want to be triggered and sensitive to life like that princess was. By contrast, imagine Xena, the warrior princess, hacking at all that gets in her way and making great strides against her foes. In this case, our foes are those triggers and stuck emotions that stop us from getting what we truly want.

Let's continue the princess' story for our own purposes. Being so irritated at her lack of sleep and knowing that her magical wishing wouldn't change her reality, the princess focused on her task at hand and mightily tossed all the mattresses and eider-down beds into the corner of the room so she could finally understand what was beneath them. Toward the bottom of the stack, with perspiration on her brow and feeling aches in muscles she didn't know she had, she uncovered the culprit. "Aha!" she exclaimed in excitement. On the floor lay a tiny pea. She had found it—the root cause of all her suffering. What a wonder that this little thing could influence all that was above in the ways that it did. Seeing it finally for what it was, she then removed the pea from its original hiding place and set it aside, letting go of her anger over her sleepless nights and instead focusing on the future nights of blissful sleep she knew she would now have. She then stacked the mattresses and beds up again and slept very soundly that night and every night since.

We all have our old stories that come from the past in the most unsuspecting times and places, just like that pea symbolizes. And when we are ready, when it gets frustrating enough or we are, for some reason or another, inspired enough, we are finally ready and willing to dig down through the layers to see what lies beneath; when we find it, we thank it for all the good it has done in our lives (because it kept us safe and alive), and then we let it go.

As you now know, those "peas" are installed before the age of two when our organismic rights get interrupted or misinterpreted. From then on, our radars scan for and pick up on what we have survived in the past to replicate just that same experience. Those choices made then were the best options at the time and served us well, until they no longer did. When working with a client, I am looking for that root cause that is coming through in the current state of events that has my client all twisted in knots. Even if the client can only track a certain feeling she wishes to shift in a given situation, whatever is discovered holds enough information to commence the process. Your body, brain, and soul hold a lot more memories than you imagine they do. No matter what, some part of you has stored the imprint beautifully. Once we find it, it can be teased out and released with honor and respect.

What We Survive, We Recreate

If a child is abandoned by a parent, that child will likely, even if unknowingly, find just the right relationships that will evoke feelings of abandonment. If a child grew up to be praised only for a particular thing, then that child will be more likely to do that thing and even grow to like it. The praise is the reward and the action survivable. If a child grew up in warlike circumstances, it will be more difficult to find peace and calm later in life if comprehensive healing has not occurred. Let's look at a few examples.

Escape from Camp 14 by Blaine Harden tells the remarkable story of Shin Dong-hyuk, a young man who escaped a "total control zone" internment camp in North Korea, where he was born and raised. After finally escaping successfully on his third attempt, his long arduous journey led him today to live in Seoul, South Korea, where he is part of a powerful human rights movement to help others. Because of all the traumas he endured for so long, being brutally tortured and being forced into impossible choices to survive, how could he feel safe being in a long-term relationship, where there is intimacy and things that he either never experienced or had ripped away from him? In an interview, he revealed that he was, up to that point, not truly comfortable being in an intimate relationship, despite having tried, and he tends to keep to himself and his work.

Buck Brannaman is another example of how the past affects our future. He was born in 1962 in Wisconsin and learned to have an amazing grace and communication with horses. He was featured in the movie *Buck* that won many prestigious awards, including at the Sundance Film Festival in 2011. He and his brother were trick ropers, and they had been on television since Buck was six years old. Their father was their agent and tried to motivate them to do their best by being horribly abusive. They were later placed in foster care. Buck turned to horses. Today, he shares with others why horses do what they do so we can be in a more graceful union with them. Buck notes that, "Abused horses are like abused children. They trust no one and expect the worst. But patience, leadership, compassion and firmness can help them overcome their pasts." Buck is married with children, but his work takes him away from his family a large amount of the time for clinics and lectures. Like Shin, he has admitted to being more comfortable on his own, and he is okay traveling as much as he does, despite how much he loves his family.

These two examples show something called the Isomorphic Structure. That which we survive is necessary for our survival. "It's not worth it to try something new because I might not survive it." Our brain only gets us so close to the barriers before we back off from them. In neurological terms, when we get input through our senses, it gets disseminated and processed into three areas, the limbic system, the cortex, and the "critter brain." The cortex, our physical brain, is where we make meaning out of all that comes into our experience. The limbic is responsible for our emotions, our feelings of safety, and our wellbeing. The critter brain is the oldest part of the brain, called the reptilian brain, and it is responsible for our most basic functions of survival, the five fs: fight, flight, freeze, fornicate, food. Shin escaped from his torture, but it was also the only place he knew, so he now helps others in similar situations. Mentally and emotionally, he is still running in the patterns that he knows so well. The current experience is mirroring the imprint. If you look all over the world in many professions, people are doing just that. In the medical field, you will hear over and over again that the person chose the profession because of a hardship or trauma he witnessed and experienced that stuck with him, and he doesn't want that experience to happen to others because it was so traumatic. Nevermind the fact that such people keep themselves surviving their own experiences whenever they walk through the hospital doors to go to work, every single day.

Although our experiences are multi-layered and quite complex, we can still relate to the imprint differently and shift our relationship to it as adults. With the appropriate guidance, we can begin to challenge the memories and enduring experiences more objectively and thus shift our perspectives about that original experience. For example, if an adult comes to me and explains she has had a very traumatic experience with an authority figure in her life, and she is still very triggered by it, we will imagine a *huge two-inch thick* wall of Plexiglas between us and the offending imprint. We perhaps turn the image or scene to black and white, fuzzy even—whatever is necessary to begin creating the feeling of safety. If that's not enough to feel safe, then we can pop out of the person watching that scene and sit behind the person twenty rows back. Then we can pop out of that person and watch him or her watching that person watching the scene. Nothing in the room has changed, but the person's experience of being able to witness it in a very safe way is useful for the next steps.

Once safety is established and we understand that we can manipulate (with respect) the original experience, then our brain is already beginning to imagine it *can* be safe. Even a moment feeling safe while watching a black and white and blurry scene through Plexiglas is a relief for the critter brain that has been on high alert for a very long time. Teasing apart the belief structure with more questions such as, "Are *all* authority figures like that?" "How do you know they are?" will give more power, ease, and objectivity. These questions are merely offerings for the system to accept or reject as the system sees fit. The adult who is sitting with me here and now—and not in the triggered state—has a greater number of resources than the child who had the experience and created the trigger response for protection. When we can pop in and out of those two states, and bring in new ideas and resources acceptable to both the adult and the child, the brain and system will be updated and the adult will start operating in a more integrated way.

"Most people are managing their suffering
rather than mastering their fulfillment."

— Anthony Robbins

Healing Your Past: Emotional Traumas, Anxiety, Fear, and PTSD

A close colleague of mine, Mike Peterson, the founder of the San Francisco Center for Emotional Healing (sfceh.com), has been very successful with rapidly healing childhood and adult emotional traumas—from fears, phobias, and anxiety to Post-Traumatic Stress Disorder (PTSD). Mike describes the effects of emotional trauma as a scale, or continuum:

> Because everything we choose to do or be is processed in our brains, every emotion or motivation, is driven by past learning. Our brain cannot help but compare everything we want to do or have to past experiences and determine whether it's safe or not. Some people describe this as their "inner parent" or "that same inner voice" that tells them whether they should do it or not.

He goes on to say:

> It turns out that no matter what your upbringing or life was like, your emotionally traumatic experiences are a part of *everything* you do, every day. From simple anxiety around riding a bicycle or whether you procrastinate balancing your checkbook, to the extreme end of the scale where people are suffering from PTSD—your brain processes it all the same.

We are often almost completely unaware of this because we go about our daily activities without thinking about it. But for those with PTSD, generally speaking, it means that for more than thirty days after a traumatic experience like sexual, physical/emotional abuse, a car accident, a war, etc., the person has some specific, pronounced symptoms.

Someone who has suffered or witnessed a traumatic event, or sometimes even just worried intensely about the welfare of others, can experience intrusive, negative thoughts. The more he or she tries to suppress these thoughts, the worse they may become. Commonly, people will avoid certain types of activities and locations. They avoid large crowds or open spaces. For example, veterans frequently report that they avoid going to stores, movie theaters, busy shopping districts, concerts, etc. Some people have to work inside a building versus outside, or they need to stay away from where there might be gunshots, firecrackers, or fireworks displays. Loud noises are simply not tolerable.

PTSD will alter one's mood and ability to think. Children with PTSD often have trouble concentrating and functioning in school. Adults tend to be more irritable or angry and withdraw into increasingly smaller groups of friends and family.

Since our brain is constantly checking to make sure we are safe in whatever we are doing or considering doing, PTSD creates a constantly heightened state of fight or flight arousal and reactivity. My clients describe it as "having a short fuse," being "jumpy," or constantly fearful. Some people literally rush home from work and will not leave for almost any reason.

These are classic stimuli and response triggers. You might ask yourself: "Who or what triggers me? Do I become angry, scared, or have trouble sleeping without background noise? Does the screeching of tires, the sound of firecrackers, or the fear of being around people I don't know make me sweat or become so anxious that I jump, startle easily, or have to leave to catch my breath? Do certain people or types of people set me off?"

Living with Anxiety, Fear, and Trauma

Everyone who walks the face of this planet has experienced fear. It's how we learn to be safe, like not walking out into traffic, stepping off of ledges, or sitting comfortably in a burning building. It's how we adapt to our world, and it's why we have evolved to sit at the top of the food chain.

But these experiences can actually hurt us, both emotionally and in getting what we want: love, financial security, better health, lower weight, etc. The frustrating reality for adults trying to change is that we don't have what we want because of both subtle and obvious fears.

By contrast, I invite you to think of some of the things you do effortlessly. Do you think about starting your car on a cold morning, try once, fail, and give up? What about the things your friends and family say you are good at doing? And do you automatically become afraid of doing the things you do so easily, like tying your shoes, taking a shower, or eating your favorite food?

Such situations are frustrating because we want to change our habits. We want to take a risk and go after a better job or a better relationship, but we avoid those things—or we start and then stop. Then we might get depressed or angry with ourselves. "How could I procrastinate so badly?" "Why am I such a failure?" "Why can't I stop eating too much?" These are all ways that we try to explain why life is the way it is.

To top it all off, our friends, family, and coworkers try to support us with "good" advice. We know they have the best intentions when they tell us to, "Just let go of your fear!" Or when they say all you have to do is "Just get over it" or "Just stop it!"—which is almost the worst advice anyone could give, yet so many do and with the best intentions.

If only it was that easy!

Great News About Your Traumatic Past! It's All Healable!

No matter what happened to you or how severe your day-to-day fears are, we practitioners are now easily healing them and changing lives! We are helping people nearly effortlessly release the pain of their pasts and naturally feel motivated to do without fear what they want to do.

But how is this possible? We've only recently discovered that we are always of two minds in a very specific way. Our brains have evolved over the millennia to remember certain types of skills, but most importantly, to keep ourselves alive. The reason why we can heal the worst memories is because we've discovered that each hemisphere of our brain has its own way of doing things.

114

Each hemisphere even has its own personality. This occurs because we humans haven't evolved to the point where our brains automatically complete one specific type of learning from those adrenaline-filled experiences. Without that complete learning that is taking place internally, we can remain stuck. It takes some expert help in brain hacking through conversation and imagination for people to complete the learning.

We still feel fear, loss, sadness, and anxiety from our past because the right hemisphere of our brain still thinks that our pain-filled events are happening *right now.* Herein lies both the conundrum and the solution so you can become *ridiculously awesome* much more quickly!

When we know exactly what we want, we are able to stir up those certain fears and anxieties that "sabotage" and derail us. Then we can update our right hemisphere, easily and gently healing our past so we can do the things necessary for *awesomeness.*

If we want a new job but have been too afraid to apply, we must teach our right hemisphere how to feel safe here and now and to realize that the events of the past are over. Then we teach it how to feel motivated in just the right ways. When there is no fear about applying for a new job, we can effortlessly do what's necessary to get it. Want a new relationship? Afraid that the same old thing will happen and your heart will be broken again? How about just balancing your checkbook or cleaning your desk? It's all the same thing, and our brains don't distinguish much between them.

Here is a real life example of how it can work for you.

Linda, an insurance executive in her mid-fifties, excelled in her little agency, but her career was going nowhere. She wanted to work for a larger company and achieve larger success. But one problem held her back. She couldn't bring herself to apply for any of the jobs she wanted. Why? It wasn't that she wasn't smart enough. It wasn't that she didn't dress the part. It was heights. Linda was afraid to look out of a window more than three stories high. She could get in an elevator, but she just wouldn't step out.

We easily turned off Linda's fear of heights by healing a teenage trauma. Her fear disappeared, and within a year, she had a great new job making more money—with an office in the sky. She loved looking down on the city! Her friends said she was like a whole new person!

Here is another example: Jake is a former Marine who served in Iraq in the brutal Battle of Fallujah. Like many veterans, he could hardly sleep even with a mountain of pillows and background noise from a big fan that kept his wife awake. He would pace throughout the house at night with a gun in his waistband, checking the doors, windows, and any shadows in the backyard. Protecting his family was the most important thing in his life. His sleep deprivation was wrecking his marriage, his relationship with his children, and putting his job at risk. One morning, his PTSD was triggered when his little boy was playing with a metal firetruck. He grabbed his son, rolled under the dining table, and wouldn't let go until they were both crying and scared. Jake was even thinking about how he could kill himself and still have his family get the life insurance money to live on.

Through working with me, Jake learned how to turn off his nightmares, and that, in turn, turned off his PTSD. He started sleeping and got his energy and mood back on track. He did better at work and reconnected with his wife and his children. Within weeks, his life was changed. Jake's mind had finally come home from the war in Iraq.

No matter what happened to you in your past, it can be healed. You can choose a new life that fulfills your mind, body, and soul and actually create it. When you follow the exercises in this book, you'll discover what you want and how you want your life to be. That is the first and most important thing you can do. After that, healing your fears, healing your soul, and having an effortless *road to awesomeness* will come more naturally than you ever thought possible.

If changing your life can happen so quickly, what will you do first?

Silencing the Tapes

At one point in my life, I had had enough of the incessant chatter in my head. I was in my early thirties and still trying to sort out who and what I was. My brain was so filled with this stuff that I didn't know what to do with it. I remember when I finally yelled in my head "Stop!" It felt like a huge bullhorn in an amphitheater, reverberating into the rafters and through the floorboards of my head. Then there were a few long minutes of complete silence. Nothing. Stillness. Not a pin drop or a peep from anything. I thought, "What just happened here?"

From the depths of my soul and both sides of my brain, all parts wanted the same thing and aligned together—vibrations resonated to make a beautiful shift. This process also further reinforced just how much untapped and unrealized power I had. When I finally cleared myself of all the negativity, I experienced silence. Blissful silence. I don't know how long the fears were there, but it was a relief to know that they were gone and it was just me. *Just me.* What a concept. Where did they come from? Many were created by me and installed, like taking bits of code and putting it in the hard drive, building up a how-to guide for living successfully. Little sound bites from my parents were recreated and mixed to suit my needs. Some didn't even sound like anyone I knew—and some of those were more pernicious, but we will leave that discovery to a later chapter.

We use information we learn from our families, surroundings, teachers, and the world to create our master guide. But I want you to know that this information isn't you so you don't *have* to have it. You *can* change it, thank it, and then delete it, if you wish, or you can even update it. You can really do anything you want. And it begins with your intentions. What would you like? It's such a simple question, yet filled with profound possibility. When you are able to clear out the scattered thoughts and all that you don't want from your mind, the next step is to learn how to keep your intentions focused despite what the world may throw at you.

"The ego is a master illusionist, and one of the ways it diverts your attention, from the moment you're born, is by giving you—and this calls for another drum roll, please—problems."

— Gary Renard

Shoku Rei (pronounced Cho-Koo-Ray) has the general meaning: "Place the power of the universe here." This symbol is used in the energetic healing tradition called Reiki. If you see the seven points of the spiral crossing the staff, some say they represent the seven chakras that are located along a person's spine.

CHAPTER 6

BALANCING YOUR BRAIN

"When your brain works right, so can you.
When your brain doesn't work right, neither can you."

— Dr. Daniel G. Amen, M.D.,
Change Your Brain, Change Your Life

Do you remember the 1980s anti-drug commercial with a sizzling pan and a man saying, "This is your brain." Then he cracks the egg and as you watch it sizzle, he says, "This is your brain on drugs." I can still feel my reaction as I thought, "I don't want that to happen to my brain!" As we have discussed before, how you nourish your body with food, positivity, exercise, and relationships plays directly into your happiness and productivity. But what about the parts of ourselves that are not amendable to a conscious shift or being uplifted? What about the parts of the brain that are hardwired into a certain way of thinking that leads to ADD, Asperger's, dyslexia, autism, and the like? Is there a way to work through those areas so you are not constantly battling your brain? Can we apply that knowledge to other parts of our experience? Can we master our brain so we run it, rather than letting it run us?

I have dyslexia. Better yet, I will say dyslexia is exhibited because of how my brain is currently wired, especially when stressed or tired. I think more globally and have high intuition. My right (Gestalt) hemisphere is dominant, where creativity, spatial awareness, imagination, feelings, non-verbal communications, and arts are processed. That's not to say I don't use my left side, where facts, language, analysis, logic, thinking in words, and computation are processed, but I certainly like to live on the right side. In second grade, my teacher discovered I had dyslexia because I kept flipping numbers and letters, the most common early indicator. Once that happened, my dad drew on my back with his fingers, a much-needed kinesthetic component for better integration of letters and numbers, but school still remained difficult.

While architecture has a lot to do with design and 3-D imagining, other components are required like clear handwriting, focused thinking, communicating ideas verbally and visually, calculations, and analysis. When my dad learned I had chosen architecture as my major, he said, "Do you know how hard that is?" To which I replied, "It will be good for me." On top of really loving to design, I also really wanted my brain to become stronger, more balanced, and to improve my weak areas. I needed more left brain exercise. Somehow, it just felt right, and I would just do my best with the hard classes.

My engineering, physics, and calculus classes were tough, and although I tried my best to go slowly and methodically, I would still make many errors on my calculations due to the stress of wanting to get the right answer. This resulted in less than stellar grades. It wasn't because I didn't understand the concepts. I just couldn't get through three pages of calculations without making a + where a − should go and vice versa. My eyes would skip, and then I would stress, and then I would skip even more. Those derivatives were the bane of my existence! I didn't have any of the resources at the time to help prevent my disorientation—there really wasn't much out there to help kids with dyslexia. And even if there were options, it's difficult to ask for what you need when you don't even know what it is. You think it's just hard, not that you need more tools to help you do your work. I had to grin and bear it, and just do the best I could with what I knew and what I had.

Let's fast forward to my thirties. I was working at an architecture firm in San Francisco. I kept noticing that when I reviewed line drawings, I blanked out and/or my eyes literally skipped across the page. It was frustrating and I felt shame over what kept happening. I hated to do incomplete or sub-par work, but no one was pointing out the crux of the problem. No one knew, not even me that dyslexia applied to lines and a whole host of other things as well. One evening, it finally entered my head that perhaps dyslexia *was* the culprit, so I went searching online for answers.

An online survey explained just how dyslexic I was. I got high scores! I was finally getting somewhere. Scoring the equivalent of a nine out of ten was a solid A! What a difference from my freshman year physics scores. "Yes, you are very dyslexic," it said. I felt both victorious and a little saddened. It felt like a good news, bad news scenario where I knew the answers would come, but what would happen once they did? Why hadn't I known more about dyslexia when I was younger? Would life actually get easier with this knowledge? I pressed on. A few days later, I spoke with a consultant trained by the Davis Dyslexia Association International who convinced me to do a one-week course. During that week, many mysteries of how my brain operated were revealed to me. I learned it's not just a reading problem. I learned how I get tripped up or disoriented, and what to do about it using three ingeniously simple, yet effective tools. I also learned that high contrast pages disorient me, and using a calendar with soft lines and the surrounding months helped me stay "in time." Polishing. Polishing. Polishing.

Dr. Robert Melillo, creator and cofounder of Brain Balance Centers, writes in *Disconnected Kids*, "In order for the brain to function normally, the activities in the right and left hemispheres must work in harmony, much like a concert orchestra."

I will not get into the depths of which parts of the brain do what and how, but I am sure you have felt the feeling of firing on all cylinders—and felt when you are not. We certainly don't function like an orchestra if we don't take care of our bodies. Without proper sleep, nutrition, hydration, happiness, and beneficial connections with others—everything that nurtures our bodies and spirits—and with the introduction of toxins, the body, the mind, emotions, and spirit cannot operate efficiently. Your fine brain needs to be nourished in all the right ways. When it is, watch out for the positive reflection in your mood, immune system, and beyond. There are more connections between all the cells in the brain than there are stars in the universe. But what if all the possible connections are not there and each hemisphere is not working in unison? Dr. Melillo goes on to say,

"When a certain function can't stay in rhythm, it can throw the entire hemisphere off-key, so the other side tries to tune it out. This can cause disharmony to such a degree that the two sides can no longer effectively share and integrate information. The brain becomes functionally disconnected."

Dyslexics are notorious for poor time management. Tomorrow feels the same as next week. Since math and time are of sequence, and dyslexics don't process linearly, but globally, getting to an event on time is a challenge. Being a deadline junkie had its perks because there was something anchored in space that I could relate to, especially if I wrote it down in a calendar to which I could often refer. If I could make a picture of it and imagine it in time and space, I was golden. If not, then it may as well not have existed at all. When we think in pictures, or "mental images," we process information faster, since there is more than just an image being recorded and experienced. *The Gift of Learning* by Ron Davis shares this, "In essence, a mental image is much like a single frame of a holographic movie reel, except that it contains far more than just images and sounds. It also contains elements of the entire range of human perception." With all that sensory information being experienced, it can be quite difficult sometimes to communicate in a satisfactory manner. It's like being in the middle of that orchestra but conducting only the violin section. It feels like it falls flat and is incomplete—that the experience is so enormous there are simply no words, or that the sensory input is so much that the system may have crashed.

I know many people who are autistic, dyslexic, or highly sensitive. If you are also having this experience, know that you are in good company.

One time while I was in college, our family Christmas letter said I had failed physics for the third time. "Einstein she's not…." Perhaps it seemed good at the time to downplay my otherwise great college experience, but you know what? Einstein was dyslexic, too. And he was not only an amazing physicist, but he received a Nobel Prize. I ended up being on the Dean's List two times my senior year. If Einstein could be awesome with dyslexia, so could I. As a matter of fact, so can you. We just need to understand our magical combination of what works for us as individuals, no matter how our brains are wired.

The reason I share my personal dyslexia story here is I want you please to respect and appreciate your brain and all it does for you. Don't listen to others degrading who you are or how you think. If you are struggling with ADD, dyslexia, autism, or anything else the medical field knows about, or whatever you are experiencing, don't let it scare you or make you think you are less than *awesome*. You just haven't yet figured out fully how to make your mind work for you. Your amazing brain not only calculates big numbers, but it is the center of communication, time-management, and emotions, and it connects directly to your digestion and your health. The more you understand it, the less you will be sabotaged in your daily life. *Know Thyself.*

Ron Davis, creator of the Davis Autism Approach and the Davis Dyslexia Correction Center, was born autistic and dyslexic in 1942, in Salt Lake City, Utah. He had a very loving mother who did her best to help him, but it was a great challenge. His father would grow frustrated with Ron and not know how to deal with his son. Ron ended up with twenty-seven broken bones during his childhood as the result of that frustration. Ron was nine years old before he was able to come out of his isolation and communicate with others. And it all began with making a clay model of his brother's knife.

Finding clay in the backyard and borrowing his brother's knife allowed Ron's creative side to connect and get his brain's hemispheres in sync. The use of his right-brain skills allowed the other side of his brain to connect words with language. Knife was his first word. Ron Davis went on to write *The Gift of Dyslexia,* which is an Amazon bestseller in the dyslexia category and has been translated into eighteen languages. He also wrote *The Gift of Learning,* in which he shares the tools he has created over the years to enable greater communication between the brain's two hemispheres. What humbles me about this man is that, despite the challenging dynamics of his childhood, he was somehow miraculously able to make the connection, create learning and healing for other autistic and dyslexic people, and even raise awareness and create better understanding in their families.

Recovering From or Avoiding Hemispheric Crashes

You know when you are in a spiral mentally, physically, and emotionally, sitting on the couch, unable to move until you feel better and get inspired to go out and wave your "Feeling Awesome!" banner again. Or perhaps your eyes get a little hazy, unable to see as well. This is called a hemispheric crash, where one hemisphere of your brain gets overloaded and the circuit breakers kind of switch off. Carla Hannaford, Ph.D., writes in *The Dominance Factor,* "Those senses and motor functions (physical movements) where the dominant eye, ear, hand, or foot is on the opposite side of the body from the dominant hemisphere communicate more effectively with the brain even in times of stress." She explains that there are thirty-two Dominance Profiles, that the Gestalt, or right hemisphere, develops up to the age of seven and the Logic, or left hemisphere, develops after age seven. Since this is the case, I ask you—why push math before seven in schools? The brain is simply not yet ready for it. It will only frustrate and dishearten kids and give them incorrect beliefs about themselves and the world.

> "I'm just really waiting for the music to get cooked the right way, and once it's cooked,
>
> I'm going to serve that meal that everybody's been waiting for."
>
> — Fetty Wap

When I talk about a crash, I am not saying that a particular body part is not going to operate. I am saying that it might be impaired a bit. As each body part is connected to the opposite hemisphere, that hemisphere is literally giving orders to that body part in its own specific way. The left brain is more about logic, and the right brain is more about creativity and big-picture orienting, as I explained in the beginning of this chapter. Here are some examples of what might happen in a crash. If the right eye goes offline, you might not comprehend what you are seeing or "blank" out on seeing certain things. If the left eye goes offline, then seeing the big picture might prove more difficult. If your ears go offline, then you might miss parts or all of conversations or hear sounds in a muffled way. If your hands go offline, then writing, communicating, or connecting with the world might be diminished. If your feet go offline, then your ability/desire to move about in the world seems less appealing and you move less. I hope you get the idea of how this all works.

Before we go any further, let's figure out how you are connected, shall we?

Exercise

Which is your dominant hemisphere?

L   R

Which eye would you look through a peephole with?

L   R

When you can only listen with one ear, which one do you use?

L   R

Which hand do you throw with?

L   R

Which foot do you kick with?

L   R

If you are right hemisphere dominant, your left (or logic) hemisphere will crash first. This means that any of the body parts (eye, ear, hand, foot) that you circled above in the R column, those will crash. Remember, each hemisphere is linked to the opposite side of the body. If you are left hemisphere dominant, your right (Gestalt) hemisphere will crash first. This means that any parts circled in the L column, will crash. For me, being right dominant means my right foot and right hand will crash. This means I can see and hear without problems, but I land on the couch and don't want to move in the world or create anything. Thank goodness pizza can be delivered!

The key to avoiding this whole hemispheric crash is to keep both hemispheres going so when we are stressed (when we just can't avoid stress or find balance), we can stay online by using both sides of the brain in an activity, such as playing piano or knitting—anything that uses both hemispheres. To reboot the left side of the brain, move the right side of the body and vice-versa.

The Importance of Cross-Lateral Exercises

To share an example for better understanding: I am right brain dominant and favor my right hand and foot, as well. When I was younger and started to crash, the couch was my friend. I ended up staying home and watching movies until I felt better. I never knew why until a cross-lateral exercise class helped me understand how my brain operated. Now, when the stress is coming on, I engage in cross-lateral exercises. These exercises include juggling, chopping wood, knitting, moving my eyes in a lazy-eight pattern on the wall in front of me, touching my hand to my opposite foot a few times. These exercises have one side of the body crossing the midline to the other side (imagine a vertical line in the middle of the body from your head down to your toes). That encourages the collaboration between both hemispheres of your brain. Going offline occurs rarely these days because I can catch the stressor and engage my brain before my system has a chance to shut down. Still Polishing. Polishing. Polishing. I know people who have all four parts connected to their dominant hemisphere and have a very tough time getting out of a shut down. But once you know what is happening and how to avoid it (by doing cross-lateral exercises and activities), your life will be that much easier!

"Mindfulness helps us freeze the frame so that we can become aware of our sensations and experiences as they are, without the distorting coloration of socially conditioned responses or habitual reactions."

— Henepola Gunaratana

PART TWO

THE EMOTIONAL

EXPANDING INTO
YOUR WHOLE SELF

Rod of Asclepius. This symbol represents the Greek God Asclepius, a deity associated with healing and medicine. It is used on the World Health Organization flag and has been used as a healing symbol for millenia.

CHAPTER 7

CARING FOR YOUR SELF

"Self-care is not selfish. You cannot serve from an empty vessel."

— Eleanor Brownn

Caring for the self is not just about caring for your physical body. You may be unaware of it, but there are other parts to your "self" that you need to care for as well. In total, you have four parts to your body:

1. Physical

2. Emotional

3. Mental

4. Spiritual

All four of them need care because they all work together to create your experience, so it is important to check in with each part as you go along. Continuously check in with *you*—all parts of you—making sure all your parts are all going in the same direction and in good rapport with each other. The more aligned you become, the fewer "parts" you have to check in with. All parts are already syncing up in a beautifully choreographed dance. Like water droplets all flowing downhill to become a great river, so, too, are you becoming a great river, with great power to shape your world.

Giving Self-Care

I feel this needs to be said: Caring for yourself *fully* can actually be amazingly useful. Many are told not to be selfish, to care for others. Yes, we are in a community and a family and others need our care— but we need to care for others in balance and not to the detriment of our self. I think many forget this, caring for others so much they lose their own light and power and then get sick. If you didn't care for yourself in the ways you have, you would be in a very different place now. Of course, some days you may care for others more than yourself, and then the pendulum may swing back when you need more self-care. It's a constantly evolving dynamic to find the best balance for you. But without your health, you can't give much to others.

Let's be honest here. You will probably always care about yourself more than anyone else on the planet. You are the only person who has a 100 percent vested interest in your success! You alone have your desires and the willpower to set your mind to anything—you alone are the person who can really know when you are feeling awesome and when you are not. When you are not, you are the one to seek out help. Yes, care for others, but if you don't have enough resources and self-care for *yourself*, then how can you possibly have enough to give to others? If your light is dimmed, it doesn't do you or anyone else any good. Your bright light is a gift that keeps on giving to your soul *and* to others. Let's get your light brighter and more focused, shall we?

When you care for others, always remember to stay in tune with yourself and your needs. Keep creating your own balance. The universe will help you with what you need. In one instance, I really needed not to be interrupted. When my father was very sick and in the hospital for a few months, our family went every day to offer support, love, humor, and a good meal that reminded him of what he could look forward to when he got home. It filled my days for a few months, but I wasn't going to stop going. Family members would go in at different times every day so he was rarely alone and so he felt supported. As an aside, because of all that support and love, he recovered faster and surpassed all the doctors and nurses' expectations. I worried about how the rest of my life would fare, but surprisingly, the phones just became more silent and the rest of the world responded without me having to shout out that I needed space. I was broadcasting my needs energetically without realizing it. Somehow, I put out a "do not disturb" sign, and it was heeded. And when I needed support for myself during this time, the universe answered that, too. I married that support a few years later.

"You can do anything as long as you have the passion, the drive, the focus, and the support."

— Sabrina Bryan

Exercise

If you have already been carving out time for yourself as suggested in Chapter 4, I ask you to expand it so that your everyday choice is to become more aware of how you are affected by the decisions you make. Are you subjugating yourself, or are you remaining more balanced and happy in those moments?

_____

_____

_____

_____

_____

_____

_____

Caring for Your Body

Perhaps now is a great time to take stock of your physical health. "Why is this so important?" you may ask, adding, "I'm fine. Nothing bad has happened. I may not feel ideal, but I get along well enough." Yes, that may be true, but our health is cumulative. What you do now affects your life later. If you could make simple choices that profoundly catapult you into a greater sense of wellbeing, wouldn't you just want to take a peek to see how well you are operating in the first place? Let's take it a step at a time. First of all, you *have* a body and it needs to be taken care of. Secondly, it's your body; you can't get another one. It is your only vehicle for experiencing your life while you are here. Just like a car needs oil, fuel, and a good wash once in a while, so, too, does your body need proper care and maintenance. I know many people who wait until their health is bad before they seek maintenance, but if your car is then always in the shop, how can you get anywhere or do anything successfully? It's difficult and taxing, not to mention more expensive, to take care of problems than to prevent them. When your body is not being taxed and is in a state of good health, your mind is sharper, and the rest of the parts are better able to remain vibrant and to work and communicate better together.

Fat, Sick, and Nearly Dead, an autobiographical film by Joe Cross, showed how Joe transformed his life when he had had enough of being overweight and taking loads of medications to keep himself "alive." This regimen of barely making it was not working for him anymore, so he armed himself with information and made amazing changes in his world. He learned from nutritionists what would help heal his body and keep it vital. He started to move his body more every day, with short walks in the beginning, and then he lengthened his walks as appropriate, always pushing himself a little more. And his body didn't disappoint. How did his body thank him and repay him? He started sleeping better, feeling better, losing weight, smiling more, and needing his medications less. He became his own power-house of health! When the body is in optimum condition and tended to properly, how could it be sick? There are no opportunities for that to occur.

Body Ecology Diet by Donna Gates is a wealth of knowledge on how our body processes foods and what can happen if we don't pay at-tention. I invite you to read this fantastic book. Not only will you learn how proper food combinations allow greater absorption of nutrition, but also how they create less stress on your digestion. The less stress on your digestion, the happier your body, brain, and emotions. It's all connected, if you haven't figured that out yet. You are working *with* how your body works, not against it. Even eating foods more alkaline (less acidic) will prevent certain pathogens and illnesses from taking root in your system. Like we discussed in Chapter 4 when we were considering circadian rhythms, look into the foods you eat and how much of an effect they have on your energy.

When you are eating well and taking natural (not synthetic!) vitamins and minerals, remember to drink enough water. A good rule of thumb is to drink half an ounce of water per pound of body weight. That water is not just to aid your digestion. It also helps cells discharge and carry waste away, energizes muscles, and keeps your skin moisturized. Water is crucial for good body function! Even drinking warm water with a squeeze of lemon first thing in the morning, before ingesting anything else, jump-starts your endocrine system.

Drinking alcohol and caffeine and eating foods high in sugar may seem fun and even necessary at times, but please do so in moderation. Digesting any food requires minerals, vitamins, and enzymes to break them down. If those minerals, vitamins, and enzymes are being used for foods and beverages that are not necessary for your system, you are robbing your body of elements necessary to care for it properly. Many different types of sugars are out there, and your body processes them all differently, but please know it is well-documented that refined sugars and high fructose corn syrup wreak havoc on your system. Your body may get a spike in energy from the sugar, but it will then suddenly crash. Eating too much sugar can lead to diabetes and suppress the immune system, weakening your body and making it work so much harder. Eating lower glycemic foods will make your energy more consistent throughout the day.

Proper nutrition through nutrient-dense food and supplements (as needed) is important for the wellbeing of your cells. And so is having the proper balance of minerals and inorganic mineral salts to make all that digestive process possible. Most people now know that it is important to have a little salt in the diet. Himalayan salt is one of the best out there. Why? The body must first have minerals to make vitamins or make use of vitamins regardless of the source. Himalayan salt contains the same eighty-four trace minerals and elements that are found in the human body. Peter Brodhead, CN, shared some history of how these minerals were discovered in a lecture titled "The 12 Tissue Salts or Cell Salt Remedies."[1] Brodhead states:

> The "Homeopathic" system of the Cell Salt remedies was developed by Dr.Schuessler a German doctor in the late 1880's. He analyzed the ash residue of human cells and found 12 inorganic mineral salts. He theorized that these 12 elements are critical to balancing cellular activity and health and made 12 homeopathic remedies in low potency in order to be assimilated rapidly and easily.

Cell salts are used in the basic functioning of the cells, including water balance, digestion, removing toxins, elasticity of the cells, oxygenation, nutrition, sodium/potassium balance, and more. The body uses the cell salts to rebuild the organs and tissues and they also help balance excess and deficiencies in the cells.

If you want to look and feel awesome from the inside out, then feed

1 You can read the full text of this lecture online at: http://www.brighterday-foods.com/PDFDocs/I/LR72WHCKJQ1V9LTGKT8CGWX7TM5B1NP5.PDF

your body what it needs, not just what your taste buds want. Surprisingly, if you do change your diet to more nutrient-dense foods and eliminate the sugars, starches, alcohol, and caffeine for even a week, your taste buds will adjust and you will more likely crave what your body needs. Your body will thank you! And it will work more efficiently and healthfully because it is more optimized and not having to keep clearing the junk out of your system. FYI: Before making any changes to your diet, please talk with your doctor, nutritionist, or health professional to get a baseline, and then make sure the changes you want to make are appropriate for your body.

Exercise

Write down five foods you already eat that make you feel energized and five foods that make you feel dull. Try eating more of the former and less of the latter. Write down what you notice at the end of each week.

Energized

1. _____

2. _____

3. _____

4. _____

5. _____

Dull

1. _____

2. _____

3. _____

4. _____

5. _____

It is time for you to have an honest conversation with your body. Listen to it and see what it needs, if anything. It's up to you to take care of it, right? Perhaps you think you are in perfect health, and perhaps you are. Fantastic! But if there is something physical nagging at you, why wait any longer to learn how to fix it? And if you are waiting for something drastic to happen to you, then I ask you this—what good comes to you from waiting? It will be that much harder to be on this upward trajectory to awesomeness if you are having a tough time physically. We want *all* parts and all layers aligned. That is where your greater success resides.

I invite you to go see a doctor and get a baseline of your health. No, I am not a doctor, and I don't pretend to be, but from personal experience, I have found that employing the right people to aid in your physical, emotional, and energetic health is always beneficial, even *before* you think you need it. I am of the mind always to get a baseline because I don't want to wait until it gets "bad enough" before I start making the appropriate changes. Do you have any chronic physical pains in your body? Are you sleeping enough to feel revitalized when you wake up in the morning? Do you finish your meals feeling satisfied and not heavy or dragging? Is your body in a physical state that allows you to do what you want to do? (Can you get in a car easily, walk a mile, bend down, and pick up something, etc.?) Are there any vitamin deficiencies or anything else that would be useful to know about? Are there any pathogens, traumas, or physical family history ailments that might be challenging you now or in the future? What if you could feel better now and it was a simple shift?

"The literal meaning of 'healing' is 'becoming whole.'"
— Andrew Weil, M.D., *Spontaneous Healing*

To become whole and ridiculously awesome, don't underestimate the power of eating and exercising or moving your body in the right balance. Take time for yourself to clear your head and be with yourself. Get centered and grounded in who you are and where you want to go. If you don't, no one will. Life, obligations, and people will keep pushing on you until you say "Stop! This is my time, my space, my dominion." It's okay to care for yourself, completely and totally, because if you don't care for yourself, who else is ultimately going to do it? You are in control of your vehicle—mind, body, and soul—so take care of it and become more aware of what it is already telling you.

Ancient Systems

For millennia, we humans have tried to create just the right system that helps answer the questions of who we are, why we are here, and how to make just the right choices and help us on our path. In the appendices, I have included two of these systems that have stood the test of time and are still quite useful in tuning into your body and experience. These are both the Chakra System and the Tree of Life. I will get into the descriptions in the appendices but want to describe some other systems out there that you may want to check out for yourself and use as seems appropriate to your needs, if at all. The other systems of which I am aware include the Enneagram of Personality, an ancient nine-pointed personality style diagram that has roots dating back 4,000 years and was often used by Pythagorians (mathemeticians). It has had resurgence in the last decade or two and has been used by businesses and individuals to help promote understanding and better collaboration between people. Astrology is the study (or belief system) that the influence of or correlation between "celestial observations and terrestrial events" can help us understand our circumstances. One can thus make the appropriate decisions based on that information. The Chinese Zodiac, also called Shengxiao, is based on a twelve-year cycle, where an animal represents a particular year; the attributes of that animal being expressed more prominently in that year. Suzanne White wrote *The New Astrology* and other books where she has combined the knowledge from both systems. From personal experience, I have found her books and her advice to be surprisingly accurate. The Tarot is a deck of playing cards that was created in the fifteenth century and later used for divination in the eighteenth century. It is still used today. My perspective is that with the divinatory aspects, you are picking cards to be, essentially, the source "out there" to inform yourself through pictures and support description "in here" what you need to know, or what you know already but are afraid to take action upon. Runes, or the runic alphabet, began around 150 AD. They were the basis of the Germanic languages before the Latin alphabet was adopted. As the runes evolved, meanings were attached to them; they were sometimes used in creating magic amulets and later were also used as divination tools. Like the tarot, it has been my experience that runes will help to point you in the direction you perhaps are already going so they are a reassurance of your choices. I will say also that whether these systems are useful or accurate or not, they are useful for those who are seeking them. Once a person finds his or her own true nature and power, some systems may no longer be needed to help that person on his or her path. The systems have then served their purposes and can be set aside with gratitude.

Caring for Your Brain

In this decade, we have made incredible discoveries about the brain! The field of neurology has found that the brain is not fixed—it keeps learning, growing, shifting, and changing according to new input. The input comes not only from what we experience through our senses, but also from what we eat. Andrew Weil, M.D. writes in *Spontaneous Healing* "the mind can depress the immune system and can unbalance the autonomic nervous system, leading to disturbances in digestion, circulation, and all other internal functions." Recently, it was discovered that the brain is directly tied to our digestion. This "brain in your gut," as it is called, is the enteric nervous system. Jay Pasricha, M.D., director of the Johns Hopkins Center for Neurogastroenterology, says, "The enteric nervous system doesn't seem capable of thought as we know it, but it communicates back and forth with our big brain—with profound results." With the connection from our bowels to our brain, maybe you might put more thought into eating for your brain and body, not *just* your taste buds.

Your physical body is a meter of what is going on emotionally, spiritually, and cognitively. It is up to you to take it seriously and listen to it. Our bodies are designed to be in equilibrium and in good health. It is not unnatural to do so, but once we put non-healthy things in our bodies—toxic food, too much alcohol, drugs, etc.—they will take a toll and open us up to imbalance. And when there is imbalance, there is sickness, fatigue, and later, disease. So control your fate by making more appropriate choices for yourself.

Doing the little things consistently, every day, that are aligned with your purpose and highest goals will get you to a better place. I'm not saying to go overboard, but if you want to become more awe-

146

some than I know you already are, you have to feel awesome in all ways. If one part is not well, the other parts will have to compensate, which puts stress on the whole system. Over time, that stress could take its toll. Physical health is a very important component of your system. It influences your thoughts, feelings, confidence, and outlook. Hormones, vitamin levels, gut flora, bone alignment, and other systems play their parts. The importance of creating health for both your brain and your physical being is paramount. All of these amazing parts feed off each other and can give you amazing clarity, focus, balance—and health. Find the right practitioners to help you assess, heal, and align. If you take care of your body, it will take care of you. If you don't know how to start, like anything else, start small and easy, so you can be motivated to continue. That momentum of success will feed on itself.

Caring for Spirit

Whatever your beliefs about whether God exists, or how that being exists as creation, nature, male, female, or anything else, there is no doubt that having faith or a connection with something outside (or greater than) yourself often creates a greater sense of peace within. Although we imagine we are all alone in this world, creating our path or witnessing it unfold, the element of faith is a very beneficial element. Spirit is not ego, where you are fighting for your existence, but the breath in the moment—that quality or essence that cannot be quantified in space and time. Whether you feel that your spirituality needs to be practiced or exhibited through meditation, a walk on the beach or ambling down the street and being in stillness somehow, just practice and take notice of the inner peace that unfolds within you. If you even find a labyrinth to walk, you might find it incredibly calming. With one way in and one way out, the narrow constantly bending path requires focus and careful stepping. By the time you reach the middle, your monkey mind will have been so focused on the walking that what once may have previously occupied your mind may be now on vacation! Labyrinths have been in existence for ages and have been used to calm the mind and connect with self. If you ever find yourself in Chartres Cathedral in France or Grace Cathedral in San Francisco, California, or stumble upon a labyrinth in a field, I invite you to give it a try to create more contentment for yourself.

When you are discontent, you always want more, more, more. Your desire can never be satisfied. But when you practice contentment, then like the Dalai Lama, you can say to yourself, "Oh, yes—I already have everything that I really need."

Exercise

Take a fifteen-minute walk every day and just breathe in and out, giving your ego a vacation for a while. Just experience the world without judgment and notice how you connect to things and people. Notice further that interplay, that dynamic that you may not have already noticed occurring between you and all else. Just notice and don't label. Don't dissect it. Just notice and breathe it in. How are *you* in relationship to all that is?

_____

_____

_____

When Parts of Us Aren't Even There: Soul Loss/Soul Fragmentation

A friend of mine shared her great sadness over breaking up with her on-again, off-again boyfriend of ten years. They had grown close as best friends and later as lovers, but whenever things got to a "perfect" state, he would throw up a wall and then sabotage the relationship. I felt for her and didn't understand the reason why it ended the way it did. But then she told me that his parents would divorce, then come back together, separate, come back together. They were currently separated. Any bells going off for you from what you have already learned here? I believe he was recreating what he had survived. Once his critter brain and system were in the perfect state, his world got upended. Now years older, his system will tell him to pull the plug once it feels happy or that something is too good to be true, or something of that caliber. He does not feel safe being in a committed relationship, so he does what he can to feel better. Sometimes it's *not* you! It's the other person and he or she doesn't even realize it. The patterns are so ingrained that the person doesn't even know they are there, so he or she will think surely you must be at fault. It is not necessarily true.

After this whole ordeal, months later, my friend tells me she still feels "lost," "shattered," and "hollow." When I hear words like that, I don't take them to be metaphors. I take them quite literally, looking into the soul loss or soul fragmentation of that person. Soul loss/fragmentation is just what it sounds like—a part of you has gone away, separated from your core/main self. The pain was so big, so earthshattering, so unbearable that a part splits off in self-protection. It has not gone away forever where you can never find it again, but it will be gone until you look for it and try to bring it back through compassion and understanding.

I have personally experienced this a time or two, and when it happened, I just didn't feel complete anymore. Part of me felt empty and hollow, and literally just not there, even if physically, all my body parts were there. It's an odd feeling, but perhaps you have experienced something of this sort. That part, when you go looking for it, will be stuck in time, in suspended animation, but very real and very much a part of you. To get it back, some convincing must occur because it left for a very good reason.

A client of mine, Mary, had an experience every few months where she would wake up in the middle of the night and see and smell smoke. She would look around and literally see smoke in her home for a few minutes. Her heart would race and would try to make sense of it. Upon looking into her predicament, I learned that a particular soul fragment had not incarnated with her and was held in space and time around the eighteenth century in South America. In her past life, she was a forty-five to fifty-year-old man in a wheelchair who was trapped in a house that was set on fire by his daughter and son in-law. Upon his death, a soul fragment was created and remained stuck in that place and time. It did not reincarnate with the rest of who we now know as Mary. During our session, when all the parts were reconciled, acknowledged, and given knowledge of the new time and place, full integration took place. Mary has not had that smoke experience since.

Aka Cords

When someone has a really hard time disconnecting from another, one thing I will check for are Aka cords that may still be attached between people. They are like umbilical cords but invisible to the naked eye—although I am sure there are a few gifted individuals with the ability to see them. They have varying thicknesses, from threadlike to thicker ropelike sizes, and they connect people in a strong bond. They can connect from any part of your body to any part of another's body, though often I find them connected through the main chakras[2]—most often the heart. Heart is where love is and where clinging and deep connection is. Parents and their children will most often have these cords because of the intensity and deep connection that type of relationship tends to have. People in a close relationship, whether sexual or otherwise, might have them, too. And it's fine to have them, so long as you feel balanced and appropriate in that relationship. If not, then this might be something you want to tune into and rebalance for yourself.

When the time is right for you to disconnect from someone, or lighten the intensity of the connection, you can practice visualizing in your mind's eye the other person and notice whether there are any cords between you and that person. If you cannot "see" the cord, you might just have a knowingness or a sensing that there is a tug or pull to or from that person. If so and you would like to remove it, then imagine gently pulling the cord out and letting it retract back to that person with compassion and respect. To make sure you are whole again, imagine filling up that empty space with yourself, your highest vibration, God or True Source's white light—whatever feels best and most appropriate for you.

---

2 For more on chakras, see the bonus section in the back of this book titled "Connecting with Chakra Wisdom."

Levels of Consciousness/Vibrations

As you begin to notice yourself shifting in awareness through your aha moments in life, so, too, is your vibration actually changing. Your mind, body, and soul are tuning to a different frequency. That's not good or bad—it just is. If you imagine yourself like a fine Stradivarius violin that resonates beautifully in every note, when your awareness increases and pains are laid to rest, your vibration becomes higher and more refined. There will be times when you shift while other people around you don't—those for whom you care deeply, and who may not understand the hows and whys of what you are doing and turning into because they see your actions and transformation as a challenge to their beliefs and behaviors.

Like I mentioned in Chapter 2 about those who might object to you raising your vibration, another way to look at their objection is that your change causes dissonance, two vibrations or sine waves that are just not in sync. If you are not familiar with what a sine wave is, it is simply a wave that has a smooth, repetitive oscillation. Let's take it out of the judgment arena and look at it purely mathematically. Imagine two sine waves going along, same height and length, going on in harmony until one sine wave (that's you) alters in some way. Perhaps your wave becomes more elongated, for example, and when placed next to the other sine wave for comparison, there is a dissonance; one sine wave's high is the other's low-middle. So if you imagine these two notes are the vibration of notes on a violin, then when played together, they just are not peaceful. One solution is to find a new way of being with each other that will harmonize in its own way. Otherwise, one has to move on in search of other people with similar sine waves.

Dr. David R. Hawkins wrote a life-changing book entitled *Power vs. Force, the Hidden Determinants of Human Behavior* which enlightens readers about the varying levels of human consciousness. If you have not read it, I encourage you to make it part of your library. It will help you understand even more about the Law of Attraction and the associated perspectives and behaviors one can experience when conscious and intentional about your thoughts. It maps out a logarithmic scale from zero to a thousand that is broken down into two main categories: Power and Force. He states that 200 and below are contractive states (where one is taking energy with Force) and 200 and above are expansive states (where one is giving energy). At 20, a person experiences shame and misery. At 200, courage, affirmation, and empowerment are experienced. Love, reverence, and serenity appear at 540, and enlightenment is at 700 and above. Hawkins goes into great detail about the relative experience at each of these states and the corresponding belief systems one has in those states. By using kinesiology, he has been able to determine the levels of consciousness of people throughout history such as Jesus, Buddha, various scientists, and more. He has even included the level of consciousness of various important documents, phrases, and words. If you go online and search for "Map of Consciousness" you will easily find several different versions or you can find a copy of the map in Hawkins' book.

If you think, feel, and do things that are aligned at a certain vibration, then you will attract things that are vibrating similarly. It's the birds of a feather flock together scenario. Interestingly, pathogens and illnesses all have vibrations, too. If you synchronize with their vibrations, then what's to say that you won't be more likely to become sick with that pathogen? For example, many of us have the chicken pox virus in our systems because of exposure naturally or through a vaccine. Later in life, the virus can present itself in an illness called shingles, which can be terribly painful. This virus is in your body the whole time and only manifests under great stress (and remember stress can come in any form, emotionally or otherwise). When the body's vibration is lowered through a depression of one or more of the four bodies, the body responds with a depressed immune system. What you feel, think, say, and believe all make a difference in your experience of the world and how others experience you.

Exercise

Write down how often you have been sick in the last two years. Describe your circumstances and what you were experiencing in your four bodies:

_____

_____

_____

_____

_____

Physical (Doing)   _____

Emotional (Feeling)   _____

Mental (Thinking)   _____

Spiritual (Connecting)   _____

CARING FOR YOUR SELF

Write down when you started to turn the corner and when you really started to feel better (and more expansive).

_____

_____

_____

_____

_____

_____

_____

Physical (Doing)   _____

Emotional (Feeling)   _____

Mental (Thinking)   _____

Spiritual (Connecting) _____

Kanji Dai, a Japanese symbol of a man in full height and breadth. It means large or extraordinary.

CHAPTER 8

ASKING FOR HELP/SUPPORT

"Lots of people want to ride with you in the limo,
but what you want is someone who will take the bus
with you when the limo breaks down."

— Oprah Winfrey

Sometimes, the world can feel like a very lonely and isolated place, especially when we feel scared and successfully withdraw into our own private cocoons of safety. When afraid, our energetic bodies shrink, or contract to protect our bodies. When we are in that protective mode, reaching out is probably the opposite of what we would want to do. And it's hard to reach out and ask for help, even if it's just for a hug because we might have been rejected in the past and we fear it happening again. But it's important to start somewhere—and start with what already feels safe and good for you. If you can talk to a plant or tree, go for it. If it's hugging your neighbor's dog, that dog will listen intently

157

without any judgment and only love. Sending your energy out can help untangle the tight little knot and allow the energy to flow, move, and shift more smoothly. Once it gets going and you get a positive result, that momentum will carry you forward. If you feel you cannot ask your family or friends for help, many organizations locally or a phone call away can support you. If you want it badly enough, then open yourself up just enough to let the universe help you. Make sure to keep your eyes peeled. Sometimes, help comes in the most surprising ways.

Being Part of the Universe

The Grass Valley Hospital sign seemed exceptionally bright to me as we drove by it. Although it was backlit, it just felt different, but I couldn't discern why. The three of us, my boyfriend Daniel, his roommate Mike, and I were on our way to a weekend camping trip and were ready for some fun. After we settled our campsite, we set off downhill to find the river for some swimming. There was no trail to get down, so we slowly descended the steep slope of the mountain to the water's edge the best we could. Toward the bottom, we lost traction, and I kept sliding on the duff at the base. I was gaining speed and couldn't stop. In an instant, my brain pulled out a memory of a premonition I had months ago, and I thought to myself, "Don't grab the rock! That will *not be good*." What rock? A second later, I saw it. As I was sliding, my hands tried to grab the branch above this huge rock. The rock was about three feet tall and wedged at the base of a tree, but I was sliding too quickly to grab the branch above it. My hands clasped the top edge of the rock. It held for only a moment before dislodging and rolling down behind me. "Watch out!" I yelled to Daniel, who was downhill from me.

I tumbled down fifteen feet like I was in a washing machine, rolling over the camera in my pocket—the rock rolling over my leg. A few seconds later: Thud. I landed on the beach with my head less than an inch from a boulder that could have split it wide open. My arms were numb, and I started to lose my sight. My vision became all white except for a small portion that had turned to random pixels of color. *I'm going to die*, I thought. This was the beginning of the end. I would soon float out of my body. *Is this it? Is this what people experience? Okay*, I thought. *I'm ready. I trust that it will be okay.*

But nothing happened. I didn't float away. I stayed solidly in my body. Huh, that's weird. I quickly reassessed my situation. I could only see white, my arms hurt, and I had no tension in my left elbow. It felt like my funny bone had been hit to the nth degree. I realized that all the blood had just left my brain, so I thought to lie down. Maybe that would restore my sight. A minute or two later, it did, and I sent the guys to call 911. I wasn't bleeding, but my elbow was dislocated and I was in a world of hurt—the hip to knee bruises from the rock rolling over my leg didn't feel any better. The afternoon sun was lowering behind the mountain. It was going to cool off soon. We needed help.

At this time, although I had a boyfriend and some good friends, I never really trusted people or let them into my heart fully. It just always felt safer that way. Based on some past experiences, I had decided it was just better not to let anyone in. But here I was sitting on a small beach, at the base of a steep mountain, just having been thrashed, and needing other people's help. I was about to learn a big life lesson, though I didn't realize it until a few days later. This scenario unfolded and developed perfectly to get me through a very outdated philosophy.

Mike ran up through the campsite and on to the nearest home to call for help—thankfully the house was just down the road. Mike and the owners arrived at the same time and they just happened to be the EMTs for the *entire* Yuba River area. An hour later, firefighters came down to us on the beach, and a rescue helicopter landed near us on the only sandbar capable of accommodating a helicopter for miles around. Some people a mile down the river heard about my predicament and walked all the way up to see whether they could help. Their little inflatable boat proved perfect for floating me across the river to the helicopter that took me to where else? The Grass Valley Hospital. Seriously? *Universe,* I thought, *I don't understand yet, but I get that this experience is important.*

After my only helicopter ride ever, x-rays, and a sling, I was cleared to go home. In the weeks that followed, I was just amazed at the love and support and the wonderful gifts people gave me. Without that love and support, I would be in a very different place and still emotionally quite separated. My heart was beginning to let people in. When I finally put all the puzzle pieces together, I began to think that this was supposed to happen, that I was supposed to get that lesson. I finally accepted the idea that people are not selfish at the core. Unless fear gets in the way, we are loving and compassionate beings, able to give and receive love and compassion.

Being Seen

At the Institute of Noetic Sciences (IONS) conference in San Francisco a few years ago, a man walked straight up to me at the Nine Gates Mystery School booth, and the moment I acknowledged him

160

and said hello, he promptly did an about-face and walked away with shock in his eyes. What the…? I asked my colleagues what had just happened, and they said, "He just wasn't ready to be seen." What I gather was he didn't feel safe just yet, and I didn't match his energy well enough for him to feel safe with *me*. Noted. Polishing. Polishing. Polishing.

A really great safety (and coping) mechanism for people to avoid the threat of other humans is to create your life in such a way that being seen and interacting with others is impossible. It works pretty well, until it doesn't, and unfortunately, other parts of your life suffer for it. Some go to great lengths to insulate themselves from the world—staying in their homes, ordering what they need online, and avoiding human contact until it is absolutely necessary, like a life-threatening medical emergency.

Exercise

When have you withheld love, and what did it do to the other person?

_____

_____

_____

_____

_____

_____

_____

_____

When have you kept your heart open even though you feared it wouldn't be respected or appreciated?

_____

_____

_____

_____

_____

_____

_____

Understanding Addictions

In the 1970s, Bruce Alexander, a professor of psychology in Vancouver, was studying addiction by experimenting with rats. The experiment started with the rats being isolated and given food and water with drugs mixed in. An overwhelming majority would use the water until death. But Professor Alexander later altered the experiment by building a *rat park*, plush with the best rat food, tunnels, and lots of rat friends. There was water with and without drugs available to the rats. Since the rats didn't know what was what, they tried both water bottles. The result was remarkable and is extremely important for you to understand. The rats in this rat park rejected the drugged water. They didn't drink it. They didn't take it because they were already getting what they needed. They were happy in their community of rat friends and were fulfilled.

Most people try to treat the addiction (whatever it is—alcohol, pornography, hoarding, etc.), and families and friends get hooked on the frustration of the "disease." But they are focusing on the wrong thing. The addiction is only the symptom. We need to get to the root cause of why that person feels so isolated, separated, and alone. We need to treat that, nurse that, feed that. Make that part feel fulfilled, engaged, connected, acknowledged. It may not be easy to find it, but keep reading because there are a few more resources I bet you haven't heard of yet, but that are amazingly powerful in finding the root cause, healing it, and bringing all parts of you to the present— with a lot less pain. The more you can trust opening up to the right people, the more you can make those very necessary connections. To be seen, heard, and acknowledged in all the right ways is what we all want. Sometimes, we need to reach out first, open up first. Others might be so thankful that you were brave enough to make the first move because they had the same fears you did.

What You Resist, Persists

A great image that might help illustrate the concept of how people really operate is to imagine everyone in the world has a mirror planted right in front of his face when he is born. Each person walks around with it all day and goes to bed with it at night. Many are unaware of it because it is invisible to them since they have lived with it so long. You have heard, no doubt, not to take another's actions personally, and it's true! We are all projecting our own views and beliefs onto everyone and everything around us at the same time, surviving our past all the time. We just have new people and circumstances to keep the view interesting. Since we operate under the assumption that we are talking to "others" and sharing ideas, we don't realize that everything coming out of our mouth that is attached to ego is us

163

projecting. What we react to, how we react to it, are all the imprints from long ago and far away, yet we mistakenly blame the other person. Everyone is projecting, yet we don't see the thin veil of illusion we have placed over our experiences.

Often, I see people who think their problems are everybody else's fault. They are mad at the world, mad at their parents, mad that the coffee is not the perfect temperature, mad that everyone is making them feel the way they feel, and so forth. "We are the victims!" yells the ego in an effort to survive and be acknowledged. Perhaps that anger exists because it feels easier to blame others. It gives the ego a job that seems much more fun than self-reflection and taking responsibility. Self-reflection can be scary and difficult at first, but if we can step back for a moment and see that we are actually projecting ourselves, then we can consciously begin to own our own thoughts and actions—and then really start to make lasting change. "If you don't like where you are, then make it better. Choose a different path. You *can* fix it yourself." You have that power yourself, but you have to believe it! Change isn't out there; it's in here. You can start to believe "I can be that change now."

> "You have brains in your head and shoes full of feet,
> You're too smart to go down any not-so-good street!"
>
> — Dr. Seuss, *Oh the Places You'll Go*

So if we get triggered, it means we are living in the past and trying to survive it. We are actually still holding it in our awareness. Our radar is on alert to watch out for it, and thus it remains in our experience. What a merry-go-round. Part of the solution is not to ignore, hide, or be angry at it, but to let it in, accept it fully for what it is, and let go of our attachment to it. We have to find out what energy we are putting into it that is keeping the structure and experience in place. It's like the game Tetris—the game where you turn various shapes to fit together as they fall from above and when a whole horizontal line is filled, the line gets deleted and the pieces above shift down. The goal is to eliminate all the lines as quickly as you can before the falling pieces touch the top of the screen. In life, when you can delete the lines (the things holding your attention that you don't want to pay attention to anymore), there is more space, time, and ease. You can then pay better attention to the things you actually want to pay attention to, like sitting, watching, breathing, and just being, and even things that will move your life forward in the ways you want.

You are now noticing more and more how malleable our brains are, right? What we may not have been able to do at age one, we can do at age four, and what we thought was important in high school may no longer be applicable after college, yet all these things were important for our growth and learning. Our brains adapt beautifully to our ever-changing circumstances to keep us alive and moving along. Our thoughts, feelings, and actions are also malleable. We have the power to control all those parts of ourselves—we just have to trust that we can and then choose to do it more and more throughout our lives. When you understand just how powerful you are in shaping your universe through awareness and conscious choosing, you can understand and be empowered by the fact that anything is possible. When you stop resisting the truths as they are, stop holding on to illusions held together by ego, and consent to it, change will inevitably happen.

Even though we may not have enjoyed parts of our lives, one important part of the healing process is to *consent* to the experience. Yes, it happened. Yes, I was there witnessing and being part of it. And yes, it was experienced in the way that it was. Yes, it sucked, but here I am and I survived. Imagine lying on the floor, trying to resist it and not being supported by it. The floor is the floor, and gravity is, well, keeping you there. Resist with all your might! Now, finally, consent to the floor and gravity just doing what they do and you being where you are. This letting go of what could have been and any other objections will boost you out of the past and into the present where you will be more powerful.

No matter what the outside stimulus is (and there always will be one!), it is up to us to take responsibility for our part, be more conscious of our thinking, and make ourselves less reactive and more proactive. We *choose* how to think, feel, and behave. This requires desire, training, and awareness of what is going on in our heads. If you keep resisting this lesson or what the universe keeps pointing out to you, then you will remain in that frustrated dynamic. You can't change your world by yelling, screaming, kicking, and bleating. It is up to *you* to take care of yourself. It is up to *you* to choose how you think, feel, act, and respond. You *do* have that power. You are the captain of your ship! You have all the resources to steer it with purpose and well-aligned intention.

"Row, row, row your boat, gently down the stream.
Merrily, merrily, merrily, merrily, life is but a dream."

— Nursery Rhyme

Energy Flows Where Attention Goes

When people are on the phone, watching TV, drinking coffee, and listening to the family member at the other end of the call all at once, where is their attention? Everywhere! And so the person talking is frustrated because she is not being acknowledged or heard, and the emotional connection is diminished. Conversely, if you are face to face, looking in each other's eyes, there are no distractions—you are ebbing and flowing in that magical dance that keeps you both enthralled and engaged.

As a volunteer at a marathon in San Francisco, I stood at one of the towers on the Golden Gate Bridge. Thousands of people were running past me for over an hour from both directions. My job was to be a physical barrier between those running to the east side of the bridge (the turnaround point) and those running back to the finish line on the west side. I had to help them run around the tower and not run into each other. I was one person, holding my arms out in a big L, a volunteer traffic splicer, yelling out to them to stay to the right. I mentally got big, stuck my arms out, and let 'er rip. I was paid attention to for the most part, but occasionally my mind wandered. My arms didn't slack, they stayed out straight, but the weirdest thing happened. When my mind wandered, people bumped into me. When I became focused on being there, larger than life, a big pillar post for people to run around and not through, they didn't! Energy goes where attention goes. All that is inside you flows out into the world. Like a beautiful bright beacon, you are saying who you are, where your attention is, what you believe, and so much more in every moment. It became obvious to me on the Golden Gate Bridge that others pick up on that, too.

Exercise

What are you saying, thinking, and believing that you notice others reading from you and absorbing from you?

_____

_____

_____

_____

_____

_____

_____

> "All that is gold does not glitter, not all those who
> wander are lost; the old that is strong does not wither,
> deep roots are not reached by the frost."
>
> — J.R.R. Tolkien

The Balance (or Art) of Making Choices

Now that you are learning to steer your ship with more focused intention, we need to talk more about choice. If you felt you had choice in the past and were just acting on triggers—totally reactionary—the idea of choice might be a lot for your nervous system to handle. And in all that imagining, you will probably crash mentally and emotionally, which we will call a _system crash_. (I will talk more about this later.) Barry Schwartz, a psychologist who wrote _The Paradox of Choice_, shared his perspective in a 2005 TED Talk on how too much choice paralyzes us. He said with too much choice, our expectations rise to a hurtful point. "If you shatter this fish bowl so that everything is possible, you have paralysis." Know that, as we grow and evolve, we expand our fishbowls just a little at a time until we have one the size and shape that suits our identity perfectly. If we make choices outside of our comfort zone (the fish bowl), then life doesn't go so well and we get disoriented. Life will be uncomfortable until we make our lives recognizable and safe again. Some people will just opt out of the new lifestyle—lose or spend a windfall, sabotage a relationship, tank a new job—or opt out of life completely. For some, this seems like the only option. We force our choices to remain within our realm of possibility and survivability.

"Take up one idea. Make that one idea your life—think of it, dream of it, live on that idea. Let the brain, muscles, nerves, every part of your body, be full of that idea, and just leave every other idea alone. This is the way to success."

— Swami Vivekananda

Letting Your Light Shine Brightly

As you can see, there is more to taking care of yourself than you might have realized, but you will get the hang of it. It gets easier and easier. To make life even easier for yourself, include this in your self-care: Stop trying to make everyone happy in all situations. It spreads you too thin, has no payoff, and dims your light from the sheer exhaustion. Life is not about what others want for you or from you; it's about what *you* want for you.

169

An African ritualist, Sobonfu Somé, wrote in *The Spirit of Intimacy: Ancient African Teachings in the Ways of Relationships*, "People have a tendency to stay away from emotion, so we disconnect ourselves from what is happening and it becomes superficial. In ritual, if tears are coming, it's ok for tears to be there. If anger is coming, it's important that anger come out. In fact, anger carries in it a healing energy." Although Somé relates expressing emotion without shame in ritual, I think we can apply this sentiment to the Western world. We often hold things in or don't know what to do or say in a given situation. What is important to do for yourself, however, is to allow what needs to come out in the most appropriate way you can let it come out. If it is sadness, anger, happiness, or clarity and truth, express it. Other people's hang-ups are not your responsibility, but still, express with care. Above all, be true to yourself and your path. You might be amazed at the results.

I think a lot of us fear being powerful and successful because it challenges others' way of thinking, and we fear a separation or loss from that choice. People's egos can get bruised, but it's inappropriate for them to project their frustrations onto you, so you should not take them on as your own. Rest assured that others can and do take care of themselves. Stopping yourself from being awesome for the sake of someone else does *no one* any good.

We also fear that if we are finally powerful now, we might question what we were before. But don't let the past stop you anymore. We are imagining a brighter future! You actively being strong and amazing and at your best feels pretty good, don't you think? Find your passion, be bright, and in time it will inspire others to be the same.

"You may not always have a comfortable life and you will not always be able to solve all of the world's problems at once, but don't ever underestimate the importance you can have because history has shown us that courage can be contagious and hope can take on a life of its own."

— Michelle Obama

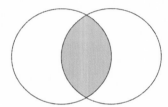

Vesica Piscis. Used in sacred geometry, this symbol shows the intersection of two circles. Literally meaning bladder of the fish, the ratio of
its width to its height was believed to be 265:153, equal to 1.73205,
which was thought to be a holy number. In the Gospel of John, 153
was the exact number of Jesus' second miraculous catch of fish in
John 21:11. Some believe it references the beliefs of the mathema-
tician Pythagoras, who considered it a holy figure. "The *vesica piscis* is a passageway to the journey of spiritual self discovery."[3] It has
been used in Rome, Greece, and Mesopotamia; it's one of the oldest
symbols known. It is used as a symbol of the Divine Feminine and a
symbol for the son, Jesus Christ. It is the basic motif in the Sacred
Geometry's Flower of Life and also part of the Tree of Life.

---

3 http://jwilson.coe.uga.edu/EMAT6680Fa06/Hobgood/Pythagoras.html

Chapter 9

CONNECTING WITH OTHERS

"Being deeply loved by someone gives you strength,
while loving someone deeply gives you courage."

— Lao Tzu

The way you think is not necessarily how your neighbor thinks or your boss thinks, and those differences can lead to lots of consternation and a lack of perfectly beautiful connecting. We all have different experiences, and thus our brains are wired differently to suit those experiences, right? We all have different or not-so-similar maps, and speak a variety of "languages." All this makes it very hard to be understood. Marriages often have this dynamic. Both spouses may be very smart people and good communicators in general, but somehow, one just can't *get* what the other is saying. Both end up being frustrated and feeling like the other is a total idiot. I have heard this time and again— and even experienced it a time or two myself. My dyslexia doesn't help matters, either, but you have to keep doing your best.

First of all, everyone has a unique way of looking at the world, right? And while that is really wonderful, sometimes it can be really difficult to come together and have everyone feel good at the end of a conversation. Whether it is at the office, in a relationship, or chatting with a neighbor or the barista, everyone wants to connect and feel awesome with one another. So let's look at some tools to make that happen. When you know and apply the tools, you can lead and engage more successfully. By creating greater acknowledgment, everyone wins and comes away happier and more fulfilled.

Vesica Piscis

Each relationship is a living, breathing thing outside of ourselves fed by our attention. When it is consistently attended to, both sides of the relationship feel balanced. If you can imagine each person as a circle, the relationship is the intersection of those two circles. It's called the vesica piscis—the symbol at the beginning of this chapter. Let's illustrate this intersection through a story. A client of mine, Robert, came to me about frustrations in his marriage. "I can't take it anymore," he told me. "I am beside myself, and I don't know what to do." When I asked how he kept his boundaries and awareness in the relationship, it took him a minute to remember how he had slowly given his power away. I told him to imagine a circle around himself and to see where his boundary was in relation to his spouse. It was right next to him, not at an appropriate distance for him to be his own person; the location of it was ultimately in his control. He had suffered a stroke a few years earlier, so with all the healing that captured his attention, he found it difficult also to pay attention to his part in keeping up the relationship. Once he began paying more attention to keeping his boundaries and feeding the relationship, a smoother ride followed.

I heard a story once that illustrates how our perspective affects our relationships: A man was walking into a new town, quite tired of his old one. He just wasn't happy there. He looked around and found an older man busy at his work and asked him, "Is this a good town to settle down in? Are the people nice here?" To which the older man replied, "What were the people like in the town you just left? You will likely find just the same type of people here as in the town you came from."

All of our relationships have their own balance; we are fed differently by each. We see what we want to see. Some people give more, some take more, and it is up to you to be aware of how they feed *you*—and whether they really give you what you need. Take occasional stock of your relationships and how they serve you so you can keep feeding your soul and not your ego. Stephen R. Covey writes in *The 7 Habits of Highly Effective People*, "Seeking to understand requires consideration; a seeking to be understood takes courage." When you are in that conversation, both giving and taking, listening and being heard, the conversation naturally ebbing and flowing, both parties have dropped their swords and shields and are collaborating and reaching higher heights.

You Can't Push a Rope

A druid teacher I know, who goes to Bali every year for a few months, shared a story about Balinese culture with our retreat class one morning. He said when you visit a new town, don't try to go in and find people. Just sit at the edge and do your own thing. Whittle a stick, read a book, tie knots; it doesn't really matter. But do your own thing and don't try to do anything to force a relationship with the town. Sooner or later, people will be curious. One by one, they will come out to see who you are, what you are about, and to start chatting you up. After some conversation, when they feel comfortable, then you will be invited in.

Little kids are like this, too, and they are often quite obvious about it. I will say to my daughter, "C'mon, give me a hug." "No" she says shifting away. I'll cajole, but she will repeat "No." Then I let go of my desire and move away, saying, "You can't catch me!" Then she runs after me. What is funny, too, is if you are enjoying your own food nearby, you will have a person quickly checking out your goods and saying, "I want to try!" You weren't putting your will on the person, but attracted him to you just by being there. Doing your own thing allowed the other to choose whether he wanted to partake. Why do you think bars are such successful meeting places? You are sitting side-by-side (a less threatening stance than face-to-face could be), and you are enjoying a beverage or food or playing darts or watching a game. These actions are common to many and are easily remarked upon in conversation. There is a lot of power in just being there, doing your own thing. Ah, such is the game played over millennia.

I know many women who are hoping to settle down and get frustrated when it doesn't happen the way they want. I used to be the same way! A friend once told me when I was frustrated with the search for *the one*, "You just have to live your own life and do what you love doing." People will want to join you if they like those things, too. *The Rules* by Ellen Fein and Sherrie Schneider strongly enforces the no chasing rule. Why? People sense when you have lost your center, and if their center is squared away, there is a dissonance, a disconnect.

Where is your focus when you are chasing? It is in front of you, or out there in fear mode, not in your core where you are most powerful, dynamic, and naturally your beautiful, happy self. So when I was fed up with chasing, I completely gave up on men and took a photographic trip to Morocco for two weeks. I went to a party the night of my return, even though I was completely jetlagged. But I was completely centered, happy, and just doing my own thing. I was *not* searching in any way, shape, or form. And then BAM! There he was…. The rest, now, is history.

Leading a Horse to Water

Even very dissimilar people can come together when they have the right tools and understanding of how people feel comfortable connecting—it all comes from the critter brain. If a person seems safe to talk to, can be understood, and feels similar enough to me, the person will be more likely to want to engage. Communicating is like playing tennis, catch, or Ping Pong, so the most successful communications happen when both are evenly matched and engaged.

Let me tell you a story of one time when I had to match my vibration to someone else. I entered a bar to say hello to a friend after I had been working out. My adrenaline was flowing and I felt pumped so I was full of energy. After a short moment, I could already see his eyes glaze over and look for an exit from the conversation. I quickly dialed down my enthusiasm and began to mirror his demeanor and expressions. Soon enough, he was more dynamic and we enjoyed the conversation for a good long while. If I hadn't shifted, the conversation would have been very brief indeed!

Pacing

Think of a good conversation as being like a game of ping pong. In fact, let's call our two friends having a conversation Ping and Pong. The greatest conversations have both people engaged, happy to contribute when they feel like they are being heard and understood. There is a balanced flow helping both keep the conversational ball in play for as long as possible (because that's more fun. It is helpful to keep the pace of the ball at a comfortable level for both players).

It might go like this. Ping… Pong… Ping… Pong…

Both are sharing ideas and getting something beneficial out of the conversation. Success!

Exercise

Imagine a conversation with your closest friend. What did you notice that you liked and that made you feel good? Do you both use the same words? Is the pace of the conversation balanced? Are there constant interruptions, or is there space for breath between each speaker? How well matched are you?

_____
_____
_____
_____
_____
_____
_____

A less successful conversation might go like this. Ping lobs a nice shot to the middle of the table. Pong smashes the ball back across the net. Ping dives to the right and drives it back. Pong, eager to play, smashes the ball again to the opposite corner—thinking what a fun game this is! Ping is not used to this type of playing, but he tries to keep up. Unfortunately, Ping is slowly weakening and getting a bit overwhelmed.

Here is how it may play out in shorthand:

Ping. Pong! ping… *Pong!* ping… *Pong!!* p i n g… PONG!!!

Ping struggles, digging deep, but he is mismatched and out of sync, unable to keep up with Pong. If there are multiple rounds of this situation, the mismatch gets exacerbated. Pong eventually "wins" the game, yet Pong has no one to play with anymore. Ping is now shattered and does not find value in playing with Pong. Ping has disengaged, doesn't feel heard, and wants to find someone else to play with. Has this ever happened to you?

Exercise

Remember a recent conversation where you noticed feeling worse after you talked than you did before. Write down what you felt worked, what didn't, and what you would have liked to have had happen.

_____

_____

_____

_____

Tip

If you ever feel you are in Ping's position, here's a tip that might help you rebalance the conversation. Focus your attention on your belly and all the way down into your feet while you speak and without attachment to what is being said. This is called being grounded. If you sense that you are starting to spin upwards above your heart and shoulders, or even higher, breathe in and focus downward. Breathe and expand your awareness, so you don't get in the feeling of, "I'm being attacked" (whether it's the other person's intention or not). Calm your face; evenly pace your breathing. Listen to cues about what the other person needs.

It's always a balance of listening and then communicating back in a way that the other person can receive your message successfully. No matter how amazingly you thought you communicated, if the other doesn't "get it," or responds negatively, then try again with some shifts in content and pacing to match the other person more successfully. If you are talking to a fast talker, talk fast. If you are talking to someone who talks too fast for your sensibilities, start by matching her pace for a while and gradually slow down until you are more comfortable. See whether he follows. It may take a few times, and a few minutes, but you might be surprised by how much you can lead a conversation with subtle shifts such as this.

Here's how a learning conversation would go with Ping starting and shifting throughout:

Ping. Pong (establishing pace/words, intensity). PING. Pong... (let's try this!) PING! P o n g (oops! adjustment phase). Ping... Pong... Ping. Pong. And it rides like that beautiful sine wave. The conversation has reached a happy equilibrium point.

Mirroring Words and Body Language

Mirroring body language is another useful tool for encouraging engagement. Notice how the person you are talking with is standing or sitting. Note the placement of arms, legs, and posture. What facial expressions do you see? Try throughout the conversation to mirror these and see whether you get a more engaged result. Repeating phrases or words that stick out as being unique to him or her and picking up on topics he or she is passionate about will perhaps excite the other person's critter so it will say, "Yes! This person really gets me! I feel understood. I am acknowledged." Notice whether the other person is using more auditory words ("I hear," "It sounds like") or kinesthetic words ("sense," "feel").

Everyone wants to be acknowledged and understood, and mirroring is a very complimentary way of doing it. Beware: Don't take advantage of this to get your own way. Don't let your ego take someone for a ride. I hope you always come from a place of integrity and trying to establish a real connection. Everyone wins in that scenario.

"Instead of condemning people, let's try to understand them.
Let's try to figure out why they do what they do. That's a lot more
profitable and intriguing than criticism; and it breeds sympathy,
tolerance and kindness. To know all is to forgive all."

— Dale Carnegie, *How to Win Friends and Influence People*

Take Notice of the Conversation's Elements

When having a conversation with someone, take notice of the conversation's elements. For example:

Are *comparative* or *similarity* words being used like similar, same, more of, less of, resemble, or matching; or are *difference* words being used, such as different, distinct, other, separate, distinct, or varied?

What *sensory* words are used? Do you use auditory (hear, sounds like), visual (see, looks like), kinesthetic (touch, feels like), gustatory (taste, tastes like), or smell (smells like, scent) words? Catchall phrases that work for almost anyone are words like "notice" and "experience" because they use all the senses and leave things up to the listener's interpretation.

Toward/Away: Is the conversation about moving toward a goal or about leaving and moving away from something? For example: I'm so looking forward to my trip to Antarctica next year. (Toward) Response: I hope it isn't too cold and that you don't get stuck on the ice. (Away) If you have two people talking from different perspectives, there will be a lot of mismatched dialogue, and the conversation may be short because one or both may not feel understood.

Find your *Balance* in the conversation. Do you pause so others can respond? Are you more of a listener and respond only to direct questions? Do you dominate or overwhelm? Do you sympathize to the point of forgetting your own point of view?

Locate your *Boundaries*. Know how you are feeling in all parts of the conversation. If you imagined a bubble surrounding yourself, is the bubble taking all the space? Is it really close around you, just off your skin where you feel stifled? Or is it somewhere in the middle? (Ideally, it's about eighteen inches from the surface of your skin, which matches up with where, ideally, your aura ends. Your aura is the electrical current that exudes from your body, which, to some people, is visible to the naked eye.)

Notice *Key Words*. What words or phrases keep coming up, coming out, or seem to be very poignant for the person? "Oh, I *love* that band!" Response: "Really? Awesome! How much do you *love* that band? Have you seen them before on stage?"

Our critter brains light up and get happy when we feel acknowledged and understood. We like talking with like-minded people, and we get really happy when they mirror what we have to say and how we say it. It's in our nature! When you say just the right words, in just the right way for the other person's critter brain to light up, bingo! You are off to a more fruitful and dynamic conversation. Awesome!

Exercise

At the next dinner party or meeting, try to use the above tools to engage more successfully in conversation—mirroring body language, words, pace, and sharing in the conversation rather than dominating or being dominated. Write down what you notice.

_____

_____

_____

_____

_____

The Shell, with its hard casing to protect the life inside, symbolizes the protective aspect of love. It has had slightly varying symbolism in different cultures. Seashells were considered to represent regeneration by the Romans. Venus, the Roman Goddess of love and fertility, is often depicted as emerging from a scallop shell. The ancient Hindus have associated the conch shell with calling out to love-filled hearts and awakening the hearts of the faithful. The Native Americans have also used seashells to symbolize fertility and love.

The particular shell shown above is the chambered nautilus. It is well-known to exemplify Sacred Geometry, a science that explores and explains the physical and energetic patterns of how the universe organizes itself. Sacred Geometry is essentially the relationship between the progression of growth and proportion. Spirals tend to follow the Golden Ratio or Fibonacci Sequence in their shape.

The Golden Ratio (or Divine Proportion) is 1:1.618. This proportion can be seen in works of art and structures and designs all across the world, including in Renaissance works such as those by Michelangelo and Leonardo da Vinci's "Salvator Mundi," the pyramids of Giza in Egypt, the proportions of credit cards, and the Google logo. Some buildings over the centuries have been designed using the golden ratio: The Parthenon, Taj Mahal, Notre Dame Cathedral in Paris, Toronto's CN Tower, and the United Nations Secretariat Building, designed by Le Corbusier who was an avid user of the proportions in his works.

CHAPTER 10

LIVING IN GRATITUDE

"Let us be grateful to the people who make us happy; they are
the charming gardeners who make our souls blossom."

— Marcel Proust

Our nephew had been staying with us for a while, trying to find himself outside of his existence with family. As you know, it is no easy
task to find yourself, but it is something all of us do at some point—
some arriving at it earlier and some later. We had a three-month-old
we were learning to care for, so why not have another added into
the mix? We were happy to have him stay, and we looked forward to
offering support where we could. We had been helping him prepare
for his college experience in various little ways, such as teaching
him laundry and date-night culinary skills, but there was one lesson
that went beyond what we expected. It happened as an accident,

but as you may have already experienced, in the universe, there are no accidents.

In early spring, I sent him a blank budget spreadsheet to help him prepare for college. He didn't fill it out, even after my repeated requests. *Damn it, I'm trying to help you!* I thought. Once I tired of that perspective, I got outside my own ego. I finally realized that he was probably intimidated and didn't quite know where to start. *Fair enough,* I thought. So one day I had him sit with me to go line-by-line and figure out his budget, which was a major reality check for him, as I'm sure you would expect. He didn't realize the costs he incurred on a daily basis, and he started to freak out when he looked at the totals. As an aside, I was kind of happy with this because it meant that he was starting to see a little bit more of his reality. Even better, it meant that he was getting closer to seeing that he could create his own world in just the way he wanted.

I spent three or four hours with him, explaining a bit about financial planning, and then I sent him on his way to figure out what else he needed to figure out. Like Buckminster Fuller and my dad taught: To know where you want to go, you have to figure out where you are. Our nephew first needed just to write down what he knew.

My husband suggested our nephew write a thank you note to acknowledge my service and time. The next day, a crisp white envelope lay on our kitchen counter. I took out the card, noticed the nice gold leaf design, and flipped open the note to see the contents inside. In the center of the inside page he had written:

LIVING IN GRATITUDE

Dear Aunt Meredith,

Thank you for your helping me with my college budget.

Love,

Todd

It was short, to the point. And for an engineering student, the wobbly cursive was a lovely touch of thoughtfulness, since his usual writing was more of a sans serif "chicken scratch" (his words, not mine). When I showed my husband, we looked at each other and smiled, a little surprised at the brevity. Perhaps the brevity was due to his engineering mind? And then we thought, *Why mince words, right?* But each word captures a variety of different sensations and feelings, even elicits various memories. And as I'm sure you already know, there is a large, experiential difference between a coat closet and a gallery at the Louvre.

The Louvre delights all the senses with every detail. The scale, color, volume, and space are all elements that create an exquisite building. And a thank you note can be like that—communicating with the reader in just the right way, making him or her feel engaged and positive about you and your relationship. We understood that he was trying, like all of us, to share his feelings of gratitude in just the right words. But we needed to get him to create something closer to the Louvre.

We both agreed that teaching him about the importance of a well-crafted thank you note, how to create it, and how to get his reader to feel acknowledged and happy to be in his life, would do great things. We already had him reading *How to Win Friends and Influence People* by

Dale Carnegie, so this lesson seemed to fit right in with that. This important life skill was a very good tool in his expanding toolbox, not only so he would survive, but so he would also thrive in the world of adulthood. Why was it so important? We will get into that later….

No matter where you go or whom you meet, when a person looks you in the eye, has a firm handshake, is personable, and has an honest smile, that person exudes integrity. We had a chat with Todd later that day over a glass of wine and told him to write the thank you note again but with "more feeling." (As Christopher Walken on *SNL* put it, "I need more cow bell.") We went over the parts of a thank you note and the great rewards of giving such a unique and personal gift (offering).

Here were our rules:

- Write three notes a day for two weeks, complete with addresses and a stamp, by 9 a.m. and place them on the counter in the kitchen.

- They had to be handwritten. No cheating with a text or a typed letter.

- He had to send the cards to different people. No duplicates.

"Really?" he asked, not quite believing our new antics.

"Really. Now, get crackin'!" we said, smiling.

Off he went to purchase more cards and stamps, and we waited for the next morning to see whether he had done it to our specification. He had, and he continued to do so every day for the next two weeks. Every morning the thank you notes were laid on the counter ready to be sent out. He didn't skip one day. And they were on time, for the most part.

When we asked him about his experience with this exercise, we were expecting him to say something about how the words started to come more easily, that he was getting more comfortable with the whole process, and that he saw the various values in it. (English teachers be praised!) My husband was hoping the exercise would help Todd be an instrument of goodwill toward men—being the best he could be by showing his appreciation to others who, then, in return could reciprocate because of the feelings they gained from receiving a thank you card. That is the power of acknowledgment. There are others in the world besides yourself, so part of finding purpose for yourself comes from acknowledging others and seeing the good in their deeds.

What we *weren't* expecting was what he said next. "When I started to run out of the obvious people to send thank you notes to, I had to think about who else to send them to. I started writing teachers, friends, neighbors, and even friends' parents who had helped me in some way over the years."

And then he said, "I just never realized how many people loved me."

My jaw dropped and my eyes welled with tears. I simply did not see that one coming. It was not only the words he said, but it was how he said them. His voice had softened and come from a younger version of himself. It reminded me of a foal just taking steps for the first time. Wow.

And then I was hit by the enormity of what had just taken place. He had finally experienced the ability to *let people in*. And for this guy, that new feeling was huge. He needed much more love than he felt he got while growing up, so he did a great job doing his best to make his world survivable, even if it meant making his world just big enough for him.

The Etiquette of the Thank You Note

When I think of thank you notes, memories pop up of my mother drilling into my head the sentence flow and the need to send them within two weeks! And I used to hate it! But over the years, I tried to see beyond the fire and brimstone of potential dastardly consequences and worked to understand the deeper meanings behind her words, and for that matter, the *reason* for etiquette. The longer I sat with it, the more I understood that it is to make someone feel comfortable, or in other words, safe and loved. In the field of thank you notes, it is to make the person feel acknowledged.

A thank you note should begin by expressing the feeling of being thankful, why you are thankful, and then what it means to you, followed by something else personal. And the finale—your name.

Aren't Thank You Notes Old-Fashioned?

Think about it: Is gratitude ever old-fashioned? Will you never thank your coffee barista or the person who holds the door for you or helps you pick up some dropped item in the parking lot...? Gratitude is *everywhere*, and it needs to be celebrated more. And the more it is celebrated, the more connection we will have, which is, frankly, what we are lacking most in modern society.

What Stops You from Writing the Note in the First Place?

My father once told me a story he heard about Sir Winston Churchill. It goes something like this: Sir Winston Churchill is sitting in a garden in London, staring at a blank canvas upon his easel. A woman walking by stops, looks over his shoulder, and asks, "What are you doing?" "Well, can't you see I'm painting?" he says. She looks again at the blank canvas and replies, "No, you are not." She then takes his paintbrush, puts paint on it, and throws a big stroke of color across the canvas. Satisfied, she says, "There! Now, you are painting!"

Can't find what to say? Start writing on scratch paper, or even in your head, thinking about what you want to say. If that doesn't come easily, look into yourself and get to the heart of the matter. What are you grateful for? What does that gift mean to you? Who made you feel loved and appreciated and seen? Once you figure that out, the words will come out more naturally. In other words, don't work from the outside in; work from the inside out. Start with the heart.

Scared to have someone read it? Yes, to have someone else read your heartfelt thank you can be scary, but…don't worry; the benefits will repay the risk even if you do not see the results immediately.

Other fill-in-the-blank reasons for writing thank you notes: If you have something important to say, say it! Stop your excuses and just start writing. And think of it this way—on one hand, it's just a thank you note, and on the other hand, it's just a thank you note. Besides, I have never heard of someone saying to someone's face, "That was a horribly constructed thank you note." And if someone does, it's time to reevaluate the benefit of that relationship and move on.

And if you didn't know, Sir Winston Churchill became quite a painter. And like him, you just have to start with the first stroke of the pen. Let's get on with it.

Writing Excellent Thank You Notes

A tennis student, who was frustrated with his backswing, told his coach he would never have a great backswing stroke. "Well, how would you want your backswing to look and feel if you *could* do it?" the coach asked. The student stepped in, swung his racket with perfect motion, pace, and finish, and then looked at his coach in anticipation. "Too bad you can't do it that way," the coach replied.

You know the saying, "Practice makes perfect"? I think it's a great concept, but I want to amend it because it feels incomplete and a bit inaccurate. If you keep practicing anything in a way that is less than *your current ideal*, then you are building that imperfection perfectly into your practice. The same is true in writing your thank you note. If you focus on your errors, then your notes will be full of errors. If you want to have your letter aligned with its true purpose through conscious writing, then breathe in, let it out, and proceed to execute with precision, levity, and focus.

Even more so, don't aim for *perfection;* aim for *excellence.*

Perfection inherently has a stigma that says if it's not perfect, it's crap, and that's quite a load to carry and stress that just shouldn't exist in the human race. Period. Excellence brings up feelings of alignment, inspiration, and a greatness that the word perfection never could. Perfection is clingy and hard cliffs. Excellence delights and dances into the heavens.

Think about these scenarios before beginning your excellent thank you note:

- If your writing begins a little illegibly and squiggles all over the place, take your time so you can write legibly. Imagine you are already writing as smoothly as a master calligrapher. Every time.

- If the spacing of your letters and words makes your letter confusing to read, breathe into the idea that you will take the space needed to write with just the right spacing. There is always more paper to write on. Add more stamps on the envelope if need be to compensate for the extra page. Every time.

- If the words are not flowing on the page, but begging to be let out, and they come out in a jumbled mess, know that you can always destroy the original rather than send it. Set it aside, rip it up, burn it, whatever! The past is done. Begin anew. There are a million opportunities to get it just right until you finally deem it ready to be mailed. You are in control.

- If the words are flowing, the writing is legible, and it ends up being so eloquent and perfect that you cannot believe it—success! And if you can't imagine it was you who wrote it, sit in front of the mirror when you are done and read the letter to yourself. Apparently, you need to hear the wisdom in those words firsthand.

Through all the bumbling of even the best thank you note writers in history, it is important to note that the receiver of your very special message is delighted that you see him or her in such a special way—in a way no one else can. What a blessing.

Getting Started

The Tools:

Imagine having over twenty different kinds of paper, card stock, you name it, for thank you notes. Yes, you read that right: twenty. Each piece has a different weight, color, and texture, and if there is text and/or graphics on it, that's a whole other ball of wax. The color, font, and everything else make a unique impression on the reader. My oldest brother knew a woman with just such a treasure trove of paper stock. She understood the value and meaning of each piece she was creating. As a fine craftsman, she was creating a masterpiece.

The paper, the pen color, the font, the spacing, the punctuation, the grammar, and yes, even the stamp…all of these marry together to create the perfect experience for the reader—to convey a feeling that you are truly trying to elicit.

As a gift to my husband for our first anniversary, I bought him business stationery from a very reputable and well-known paper company. The thick, heavy textured cardstock in crème with crisp cut edges was the perfect backdrop to the deep rich blue font of his name at the top. It reminded me of the font on U.S. currency. He's a finance guy, so it made sense. Without words, the stationery conveyed who he is. He is strong and approachable, classic, refined, but not fussy. Think James Dean meets Howard Hughes. What is the proof in the pudding? He gets compliments on his stationery all the time. So, apparently, it makes a difference.

All this is conveyed with paper, fonts, and color? Yep! And that is why there is so much attention paid to the details of a business card. In this case, your thank you note is *your* calling card.

Remember the purpose of the note: Thank you notes are about re-lating to one another and keeping or enhancing a bond between two people. By acknowledging someone and his or her efforts, you are also sharing that you see that person's heart. Since the person went out of his or her way to do something for you, it is up to you to see that and bring it full circle.

Between two people in a relationship, there is a space that is culti-vated and grown by both. Like a plant, that space needs proper care to grow and keep healthy. A thank you note is one of those elements.

Regardless of whether your thank you note is to a CEO or a third cousin you rarely see and dislike, the reader needs to come away with an experience, too, and we hope it's a happy one! If the reader never gets that feeling, then what really is the point? What are you doing to keep the relationship moving?

To Whom Do I Send a Thank You Note?

You can send a thank you to *anyone* for *anything*, big or small. It can be to a neighbor who lent you a cup of sugar, to a teacher helping you after class, or even to a nurse or doctor caring for a loved one.

In business, if you started sending out thank you notes as part of your system, how much more business do you think you could gen-erate? Whether you are starting your business or not, the relation-ships between you and your vendors, clients, or potential boss are all important and should be kept in good standing and rolling along.

If you just moved into a new home, you could create closer relationships with neighbors by thanking them for their lovely welcome. Thank family members, the letter carrier, even an editorial writer for something that has moved you. The possibilities are endless!

Thank you notes can be used to cheer someone up. Without the person ever having to know your true intentions, writing a little note of, "Thanks for being you," or "Thanks for sharing with the world your cheerful outlook," can help a person more than you know. Not everyone is perky and up all the time, right? Not everyone is smiling on the inside when smiling on the outside. If the inspiration strikes you, don't think, just send the person a note.

Exercise

Write down the names of twenty people you know from your past or present to whom you would like to send a thank you note (or even someone whom you think could use a thank you).

1. _____

2. _____

3. _____

4. _____

5. _____

6. _____

7. _____

8. _____

9. _____

10. _____

11. _____

12. _____

13. _____

14. _____

15. _____

16. _____

17. _____

18. _____

19. _____

20. _____

How Gushy Do I Make It?

The first time my sister-in-law's sister, Theresa, sent me a thank you note, it made me almost uncomfortable with its overflowing gratitude. I had never received such a glowing, all-encompassing thank you card before. It was a little overwhelming to my system. But then, as I read it further and got in touch with who this person was and the words she wrote, it made me cry. Her heart jumped beyond that ink, off that page, and wrapped me up in a big bear hug. It was *beautiful*. Her poignant descriptions and prose touched me deep inside and became part of me—and that's the whole point.

If you are still feeling unsure about the length of your note, then knowing your audience will help. Feel into your knowing of this person and edit or expand without losing who you are or what you are trying to convey. Whether long or brief, whatever it takes for you to express fully what you are saying is exactly how long it should be.

Unintended Consequences

Since strangers rarely write thank you notes to one another, sometimes a thank you note may be perceived as an overture to wanting to move the relationship to a more personal level. If you think your note could be perceived that way, make sure you write it with sincerity, but without such overflowing prose that it might lead someone on. And if you didn't write it that way, but the person misunderstands or keeps misunderstanding, it is that person's issue and has nothing to do with you. Let the person go gently on his or her way so as to minimize further confusion or hurt feelings.

Thank you notes stir up emotions, and they are so powerful for that reason. They can elicit a soft smile or touch us deeply, and they can even shed light in places that have been shut up tightly due to past pains and traumas. Sharing your gratitude with someone can have a wonderful result; it can let the heart heal in unexpected ways and pave the way for even more love in the future.

I bet you are thinking, *Wow, I didn't know that a thank you note could do so much!* Yes, it can, but why not experience it for yourself?

Your Challenge

The challenge is to write and mail three thank you notes a day for two weeks.

They must be handwritten.

The Evolution of *You* During the Challenge

No one can know what will happen exactly when you take this challenge, but I'm sure it will be something. To me, gratitude in any form takes you out of your own ego. It allows others to see you as you would like to be seen. Another benefit of thank you notes lies in learning how to be *present.* If you are looking for a meditation, perhaps this practice could be something you pick up to ground yourself and to feel more like a part of the world and essential to it.

Beyond the Challenge

Regardless of whether you take this particular path to gratitude or not, imagine where in your life you can find yourself being more grateful and allowing others into your heart and your space. It's a brave action but filled with so much benefit.

Final Thoughts

Write a thank you note to yourself, in the third person.

We rarely, if ever, acknowledge ourselves for all that we do. We are busy making a living, learning how the world works, taking care of others, ad nauseam, but aside from taking a little vacation or getting a massage…when do we really see ourselves and give a little gratitude? Look at all that you have accomplished to get here. It's incredible if you really think about it.

So write yourself a letter, and give yourself enough space and time to do so with no interruptions. When you are done, don't read it right away, but keep it somewhere safe to let it percolate for a while, maybe a week or two. (The magic of this exercise is working on the inside, on a subconscious level.) When the time is right, read it to yourself in front of the mirror. Not the bathroom mirror, but where you can be comfortable and just sit and read. As an example, here's one I wrote to myself:

> Dear Meredith,
>
> I am so grateful for "you," for all that you are, and for all you have done. I think about all that you have been through that has brought you here, and I can't believe you made it. And it's only getting better. There were plenty of times you got

scared about the next step and you hid inside of yourself, hoping no one would see you, but you kept going, clinging to all the things that would lead you out of those darker moments.

You kept moving, step by little step, and the little bits of happiness and trust started to connect with other moments of happiness and trust. Sure enough, over time, you made it here. I now sit here in awe and so amazed at this wonderful place you ended up. You are more confident, happy, calm, peaceful, and excited about the future. What an adventure it all is! Wow.

There were twists and turns, triumphs and failures, but through all of it, you came through. I am so blessed to be here, in this place, with the wonderful people in my life, and every moment filled with such happiness and gratitude, all because of the great strength I didn't even know you had. I wonder what will be next? I can't wait!

With love and humility,

Meredith

PART THREE

THE SPIRITUAL

AWAKENING INTO
YOUR ESSENCE

ༀ

Symbol Hum from Buddhist Teachings. The Five Wisdoms are expressed by the Five Transcendental Buddhas. The five wisdoms are:
the all-penetrating void in the middle, and the four emanations that
surround and mirror wisdom (east), equality (south), magical perception (west), perfection (north). They correspond with the five elements: ether, air, fire, water, and earth.

CHAPTER 11

ALIGNING YOUR ENVIRONMENT

"Sometimes when things are falling apart,
they may actually be falling into place."

— Anonymous

Now that we have talked about becoming more awesome on the inside, we need to talk about what's going on outside—your environment. Never underestimate the power of a properly energized, inviting space to enliven, empower, and support. Whether it is at work or at home, the space around you influences your experiences, positively or negatively. If it is filled with clutter, mismanaged, and untended, the energy can become stagnant and drain your system. The more stagnant it becomes, the more stagnant *you* can become. Where you spend your time actually does have an effect on your life and wellbeing.

If the environment is bright, organized, and balanced in color, materials, and furniture, you can become happier, more productive, and more empowered. It can really feed your soul and be a wonderful advocate for you. Why do you think restaurants spend so much money to create the perfect ambiance? It's not just to be visually pleasing; it must *feel* amazing for you to want to spend your money there. Make sure that each space is designated properly for its individual use. The living room should not be a bedroom, playroom, library, and workout room all in one. When there are too many uses, the intention and focus gets scattered. With the scattered intention, people in that space will feel less comfortable or scattered themselves. That room doesn't know what it wants to be. As you remember, Louis Kahn asked his students, "What does the brick want to be?" If you use the characteristics of the brick to its highest and best use, it will resonate beautifully in its environment and people will respond in kind. Each space needs to *know what it is* so it can cohesively resonate its focused energy out into the world.

Imagine your home being in a river of energy. Energy flows through the front door and into the hallways and rooms accordingly. See where it eddies around seating areas, pools in cluttered corners, and flows more quickly down hallways and stairs. Notice where the energy jolts, gets stuck, or feels uncomfortable. Make the appropriate shifts to move furniture and declutter. If you are looking to sell your home, paying attention to the alignment and balance of the energies will greatly help the impressions and feelings people get from the home. If you don't know what you need, or you made the first pass and there is still something amiss, it's time to call in the professionals.

ALIGNING YOUR ENVIRONMENT

Energetic Clearing

Our physical environment is not only objects placed in space; the objects around us are dynamic and absorb the energy of people and events around them and even exude their own. An imprint occurs, like a thumbprint left on a glass, and if you don't clean it off appropriately, the oils will remain there indefinitely, long after the finger that made the print is gone. Also, the more dynamic the energy, the bigger the effect. Great emotions amplify the imprint and send out those vibrations, like a radio never turning off. It keeps sending out its signal until it is reset to neutral by proper intention, care, and focus. If negative events keep happening over and over in a place, the sensation can become thick like grime or dirt. On the positive side, imagine Times Square in New York. It will probably have a high pumping party-like vibration even if you turn all the lights off and everyone goes home. There is an imprint on everything, and it can play on our experiences wherever we go.

I got into the work of clearing energies from buildings, places, and people when I met my Huna teacher and now friend at a retreat. We will discuss more about Huna, which is Hawaiian Spirituality, later in Chapter 14. The work piqued my curiosity so much I ended up training in it. My business, Realm of Intention, was born soon after. It is now a tool I constantly use in my work with clients and is immensely helpful. When the energies confound and even scare the inhabitants, I am hired to clear, realign, and calm the energies, with the utmost respect, whatever they are. The energy can be from a massive energy shift, such as a death, murder, or huge fight that occurred there, or it can even be from lay-lines that naturally occur from the magnetic field in the earth. Let me share a personal example to make this better understood.

When our house had been partially gutted, my husband was still feeling a little unease in our home. He couldn't pinpoint what the issue was. (He loved the home!) Structurally, it was all sound; he just didn't emotionally feel comfortable there at night when we were looking at the day's progress. His concerns focused primarily around the staircase, which rested in the middle of the house. He wasn't quite sure how my Huna and intuitive skills would make those stairs feel better, but since I do energetic clearings for clients, but he trusted me to take care of it. The whole house felt great to me except for those stairs. I definitely felt it, too. Something was off and it needed to be cleared. Waving some smoldering sage was not going to cut it for this job. My colleague, Lisa Winston, a Feng Shui consultant among other things, came over to help us understand our home better and to see whether we needed any tweaks. She came back with a report saying that the alignment and design were pretty perfect according to the bagua map, except for the funkiness at the stairs and in the wealth corner of the bagua map, which turned out to be our master bathroom.

The Feng Shui Bagua map is comprised of nine squares, in a 3x3 format. The squares are:

1. power/wealth

2. fame/reputation

3. love/marriage

4. family

5. health/wellbeing

6. children/creativity

7. growth/knowledge

8. career/work success

9. travel

Each square has specific colors and qualities associated with it. When you lay the map over the floor plan of your home, you can notice what rooms fall inside each of the squares and begin to reconcile and enhance the energies in your home to assist with the energies that relate to each square of focus in your life. There are even specific remedies to counteract any bad energy flow or disruption, from furniture layout changes, color changes, installation of crystals, chimes, or otherwise, to even moving walls; ultimately, it depends on the space and the owner's final wishes.

We tweaked the energy at the stairs first. Whenever I walked over this particular area, it felt cold and unsettled. It felt like a column of air moving upwards counter-clockwise. There were no weird sounds or whispers (though I have had that in other locations I have cleared), so I knew it wasn't a haunting or anything like that. It just didn't feel right. When we renovated more, and Lisa and I kept clearing it and setting the appropriate intention, the uncomfortable sensations we previously felt finally shifted. Marc was very much relieved and has had a very different experience in the house ever since. He finally felt the home was calm and happy. Success!

We next worked on the wealth corner of the bagua map, which was where our bathroom is located. Our wealth apparently was energetically "flowing down the drains." That is not how I want to keep my wealth! Since we were renovating and spending our money on the house, I didn't really pay the same attention as I usually do, but once we installed the solutions, I quickly became a convert to the ancient practice of Feng Shui. Now there is a big, fat, beautiful citrine that my mother, Lisa, and I all chose separately at a gem and crystal website. Coincidence? Perhaps. But I like to think that we all sensed that it was just the right one for our home. Steadily, ever since, our coffers have been doing much better and flowing in a positive direction.

A client of mine, Alice, requested her home in San Francisco be cleared post-divorce. The year before, she had had a physical altercation with her now ex-husband that almost led to her being choked. I was never told where it had occurred in the home. But as I walked through, paying attention to all I could, I felt layers of intensity come off the walls. When I asked her about the previous owners, she told me there had been three couples who resided there prior to her, and each couple had engaged in physical fights and divorced. Interesting. And what an interesting parallel we have found. It never ceases to amaze me how much our surroundings influence our lives. I always ask about the previous owners and how long they lived in a space—any tidbit to help me understand better the history and what needs to be shifted for greater harmony.

We sometimes need more than soap and water to get out the negativity. As we walked through Alice's home, some rooms were really loud and I could hear voices, while other rooms were pretty neutral. Downstairs was dark, thick, and muggy. The lights were on, but it looked so dark; the light bulbs seemed to be only twenty watts. The negativity that existed there was absorbing and covering all the light. I spoke to her about the sensations I was experiencing and shared what came to me. "It happened here, didn't it, and ended here on the stairs?" She was shocked at how accurate I was. "Yes." "Okay," I replied. "Let's get started and transform this space to get it to exude more positivity." I asked that she say some specific words of healing into the space. I was not just healing the room, I was healing her—helping her let go of stuck pain and memories.

Over and over, three, four times, she spoke them until it all just…lifted. The room almost crackled and expanded outward. It then softly eased into a neutral position and was then more available and open to new, positive energy. There was nothing left but the furniture and us. We circled to the back of the house and then re-entered the room we had cleared. I asked her whether she turned up the dimmer on the lights. She said she never touched the lights, but we were astounded by how bright that room had become. It was completely different. Awesome.

Have you ever felt your house was just thick, heavy, and uninspired? Perhaps it was after a long illness or after something majorly stressful had occurred in your life. Whenever I feel my house is feeling that way, I throw a party. It's a great way to put some groove back into the house. It wasn't until later in life that I understood why I did it, other than to have a great time with friends. It was to re-energize the place and imbue it with positive vibes. Like a fine violin, the wood, plaster, furniture, and air resonate with how the home is "played" and experienced.

Another client, Sarah, called me up once to request some help for the home her family was renting. She lived down the street from me and asked for design advice for her front room. She didn't know why she and her family didn't like to be in there since the layout was great, it had enough windows, and there was even a lovely brick fireplace. Why did they avoid using it? I walked through the house, used my designer eye, and put out my feelers. I noticed that nothing was amiss physically. The flow of the rooms in the house worked fine, but there was an underlying energy of negativity emanating from the fireplace. I told her I would be able to clear it all up, which I did later that day.

I brought my tools, my "Spidey" sense, and went to work. A few hours later, I reported back that probably someone had burned an effigy in the fireplace because there was great pain and anger residue. Normal fires don't do that to my knowledge. In a downstairs area, where they also did not feel comfortable, an older lady had died. The woman's spirit remained there, not knowing her body was dead. The woman felt compelled to stay because her son still owned the property. Oddly enough, the son kept refusing to sell the home because it was the home he had grown up in. He also talked about perhaps moving back in at one point. Was that really the only reason he didn't want to sell, or was he holding on to it for another reason? The last I heard from the client was that the son was in conversations not to move back in but to keep renting to Sarah's family. I do not know whether they were able to buy the home yet.

Imprints

Another client, Faith, asked me to come promptly to her home because people were seeing shadows on the wall and someone upstairs was stomping across the kitchen and throwing keys, although no one was up there. The home was lovely, the energy flow and layout felt fine, but something was scaring them! When I started to clear the house, focusing on the kitchen, the air pressure rose like when you are in an airplane taking off. Faith looked at me and said she needed to pop her ears. "Does this always happen?" she asked. "Not always," I replied, "but when it does, it's a clear sign that what I am doing is working. I'm glad you can notice the shift!" In a few minutes, the pressure returned to normal. She and her family have not had any problems since.

Exercise

What part of your life feels underwhelming, stuck, or less than you would like?

_____

_____

_____

_____

_____

_____

Is there a room in your home that you just don't use often or avoid? Where is it? What does that room feel like? What lends that space to feeling less than perfect for you?

_____

_____

_____

_____

_____

_____

Letting It Go

If you have a hard time letting go of things, I ask you, "What would you lose of value if you no longer had it?" Often, we hold on to things because they are symbols of memories of our relationships to people or of events that we don't want to forget. That's understandable, but when someone holds on to so many things that it becomes dangerous even to move around in the space or live in it, we then need to look at the unresolved emotional attachment that is occurring.

When there has been a trauma in the past, our critter brain works overtime to prevent that trauma from occurring again. A contractor shared with me that there are many people who hoard in Marin County. "Why so many in a concentrated area?" I asked. He said it was because those who lived in Marin before the Golden Gate Bridge was built poured their savings into helping get it built. They lived lean for a few years, hoping that it would all work out, that their money was put to good use, but it took longer to build the bridge and wealth to venture up the coast than they expected. To prevent that feeling of scarcity from occurring again, they now tend to keep accumulating to feel better.

Attracting More Positivity in Balance

Do you want to attract more positive things? Then you have to make your home and work space a place where positivity is attracted! Here are some tips to help you.

1. **When the going gets tough, the tough get cleaning!** Dirt, grime, and lack of organization are major magnets for negative en-

214

ergy. Hire a cleaning crew or do it yourself. Use that elbow grease to polish in your positivity and your wonderful new intentions for the space.

2. **Get rid of it.** Let go of what you don't use or haven't used in a year or so. Of course, there is that thing you feel guilty throwing away because of its sentimental value, or because you might find a use for it someday, but really, by the time you need it, there will be a better option. Getting rid of what you don't use will save space and the stuff will not pull on your energy and mind. Another way to feel better about letting go is that someone else may now have the opportunity to use it—it might be something someone really needs. What a gift!

3. **Put things in order.** Organize and put things in the right place, whatever "right" means to you. You will know it when you are doing it. Make it visually pleasing so your eyes can rest and your senses can be appropriately guided to the room's theme.

4. **Simplify your design.** Don't use every idea in the book in each room. Make the theme clear and then do variations on it. Don't choose ten colors. Two or three will suit you better. Please refer to Appendix A: Color Psychology and Associations for ideas.

5. **Go with the flow.** Be attentive to the placement of furniture and objects for ease of use and walking around. Don't put a couch right in front of the door, for example. It will just block the flow and those seated will have their back to the door. Put things in to allow the flow to be calm and gentle, but still moving. Use the image of the flow of a river as your guide.

6. **Balance the materials.** If you have too much glass or reflectivity, you might feel agitated or antsy. If you have too much fabric, it might feel too dead of sound and might feel suffocatingly quiet. If you have too much metal or wood…you get the idea. If something doesn't feel quite right, look to see whether the materials are in balance for your system.

7. **Delight your senses.** Install a candle or add fragrant flowers. Put the colors you love in there. Add plants to bring the outside in. Plants not only can improve the indoor air quality, but they add their own positive energy. Do what you need to do to make your experience amazing.

Respecting Your Space

When I had finished my Huna training, I was excited to clear anything and everything that I felt could use clearing. When I got to staff at Nine Gates in Joshua Tree, California, I roomed with a woman, Sarah, for a week. She ended up becoming a very close friend of mine. We shared an apartment there that had a front bedroom/living room and a back bedroom. We both, for some reason, felt really uncomfortable with the back room. When I was in the bathroom washing my face one evening, I saw a person go by out of the corner of my eye. I asked Sarah whether she had just walked by. She said no, that she was on the bed. She took her camera out and took some photos of the room. The screen showed five orbs. If you are unfamiliar with orbs, sometimes photos will show round, semi-opaque white circles. Sometimes, it is just from lens flare, but sometimes, as in this case, they were "orbs," the centermost part of an un-embodied spirit. How did I know this was not lens flair? There was only one light source, and it was behind the camera, and the orbs had no linear or symmetrical order. One of the orbs was much more opaque white than the others.

When I asked Sarah whether she wanted me to clear the room, she agreed. When I said, "I am going to clear the room now," the pressure of the room increased to such intensity that our ears popped. "No!" a male voice shouted audibly from the far corner of the room, where I had seen a person walking earlier. The intensity of the sound felt like a wave of pressure flew at us. Our hair stood up on end and we freaked out a bit. Well, I had started this so now I was even more curious about just what was going on.

I sat there, breathing deeply, trying not to panic. I settled down and deep into my feet, asking for guidance and protection. I tried another tactic. I had always been told to ask permission to clear a room; I just didn't realize I needed permission from those I couldn't really see. And in this case, apparently it *did* matter. I sat on the edge of the bed and had a conversation with those I couldn't see. I could feel and communicate with them through pictures that came to me in my head. I learned that the spirits were Native Americans—the parents, aunt, and uncle who were present in the room were trying to find two children who had died in a fire. They had died at a time of war with either another tribe or settlers. That information wasn't coming through because perhaps they didn't even know when they died.

A lot of sadness and grief was in that room. What confused me was that two of the orbs were the children, but the parents couldn't find them. I updated them on many facts, shared with them the way to get home, and how to find each other again. After a few minutes, the feelings in the room shifted down in temperature and pressure.

They were on their way to peace, and I was happy for them. Sarah and I went to sleep in the front room, and in the middle of the night, a female voice said to me, "They're okay," meaning they were in the right place. *Really?* I thought, laughingly. Then I heard a reply. "Yes, they're okay." I was still new to how this all worked. Even so, we slept in the front room for good measure.

I just couldn't believe what had happened—that I didn't make this experience up and that we literally heard the word *no* coming from a vacant corner of the room. Just so you know, not all clearings are like this. Some are more dynamic, many less, but it is still a reminder to be compassionate and use the appropriate resources to rebalance a room and offer the right solution for the circumstances.

Clearing on Your Own

You may have heard of burning sage and saying a prayer to clear a space before, but I ask that you not do it on your own if you are trying to clear out a lot of intense energy. Both sage and Paolo Santo are wonderful smudgers and have also been known to clear the bacteria in the air, but I have had a few experiences where, if I had not had my training, I could have been seriously harmed. For most places, this ritual can be just what is needed, but the untrained, who lack experience in sensing all that is going on in a space, might not be equipped to handle the unseen forces that are there. I will explain more about this in Chapter 14: Healing with Huna. There is power in intention. Ritual is a very focused practice of intention, bringing many different elements together to make change. The more focused and skilled the practitioner, the greater the effect that his or her work emits.

Exercise

Take one room that you don't feel great about and write down how you would like to have that room be in the future. Imagine what you are thinking, feeling, doing, and experiencing in that space. What stops you from already having that experience? Put a plan in place to get that done (in your planner). Be specific about how you are going to make your plan a reality.

_____

_____

_____

_____

_____

_____

_____

_____

This Pagan symbol of a counterclockwise spiral means rebirth, start-ing anew. The word Pagan simply means hill-dweller and those who were pagan long ago were part of a polytheistic or pantheistic na-ture-worshipping religion, often due to the fact that they lived and worked so closely with and in nature.

CHAPTER 12

TRUSTING YOUR OWN WISDOM

"Abundance is a process of letting go;
that which is empty can receive."

— Bryant H. McGill

I watched the movie *Holy Hell* recently, and it reminded me how easy it is to follow someone else's *wisdom* while subjugating our own. We can often lose ourselves because we think surely that someone else knows more than we do because, after all, we are just one person. We don't know everything (and perhaps feel we don't know anything at all). We lose faith that our inner compass is true, especially in times of stress. With the stress, our systems are overloaded and we are looking for relief, trying to find the best solution for our current predicament. So here comes along an "enlightened being" or someone who knocks our socks off in some special way. He or she exudes this *je ne sais quoi* that it is captivating and magnetic. That initial impression draws us in because part of us experiences an amazing feeling and we want more of it. Surely, that person's way is *the way*, so we forget to check back in with our own balance. We think, *His way is better than where I am now, so great, let me follow him.* To follow the dream and be part of a special experience or path is very alluring! Sometimes, you do truly meet an amazing person who teaches you your own truth. Sometimes the meeting is short and you have made a nice friend, but sometimes the other person's ego gets fed by your awe and adoration. This can lead to very disastrous results. Remember Jonestown? Those people followed their leader Jim Jones, resulting in the mass suicide of 918 people. What about other religions or cults that require much of the individual for the betterment of…well, for whom, exactly?

Slowly, over time, the shiny enlightened being or organization shows signs of stress, and down the path of fear, everybody is led. It is so subtle, but once things get bad enough in the philosophic/ideological structure of the leader and/or organization, some devoted followers finally stop and think, "How on earth did I get here? This is not what I signed up for. How do I get out? What will happen to me if I admit that I don't feel their vibe anymore on what they are selling?" What is the main cause of this whole slippery slope? Individuals have given up their power (yes, by their own choice) to someone else, all the while hoping to feel better and be part of something transformative. They are, thus, disillusioned and angry at the betrayal in the fallout, placing them at a crossroads because they have to sift through their own selves to find their own foundation upon which to build. Their old foundation and identity have been rocked, so they must choose either to go back to what they knew and start again, albeit much wiser, trying to take what they have learned and move forward, or to stay in the illusion and make their peace with or suffer the consequences.

We often get so bogged down by all of life coming at us that we forget or fear going inward to listen to our selves, to our own wisdom. We have somehow and for so long allowed the stresses of the outside world and our obligations to take over our whole experience that we feel small, separated, and out of balance. We are then left with little choice but to be reactionary, perhaps in hopes of releasing our own responsibilities to someone else. Life is hard; wouldn't it be easier if we didn't have those responsibilities? Sure, but freedom comes at a price. When we can let go of the fears, doubts, and tapes playing in our heads, as we have started to do in the previous chapters, we can just sit in our own stillness. When we do so, we are finally getting to the core essence of who we are, and that is where true power and happiness reside.

I talked with a woman recently who was in adoration of a female friend of hers whom she believed was a witch with some amazing gifts. She seemed in awe of this other woman. I listened to her talk for a while, and then I turned to her and said, "And? So, she may have amazing gifts of being a medium and such, but I will tell you the meaning of *witch* is wise. Yes, she is very talented in her profession, but I feel that she is one of the most ungrounded, unorganized, drama-filled people I know. Her energy is all over the place! By comparison, I have met people who practice day in and out, listen, balance, adjust, and are in an amazing cosmic dance with the world and are quite adept at it. Besides, so what if she does have those gifts? You have your own gifts. Don't worry about what she is doing. That's of no consequence. She doesn't have anything that you don't have other than the fact that she believes in herself, goes out there, and gets what she wants done. But you have that same power; you just don't know it yet."

Rather than focusing on what other people have, we need to quit listening to our own tapes and focus on our own stillness where the answers lie for who we truly are and what we can become. Just getting to that point of being in greater stillness is a monumental feat in itself, so step into that and notice what it might feel like. What's more, what if you, in that stillness, could listen only to yourself and nothing else? In that moment, already realizing that the external stimuli has fallen away, you will discover that all that is left is *you,* the you that has trusted enough up to this point. You will realize then that you have created greater space for yourself. In that you are witnessing and experiencing unlimited tranquility, awareness, and truth. The more you bring that experience into your everyday life, the more you can gain confidence in living your truth in every breath, no matter what the stimuli.

A Ninjitsu master shared with me a core principle in the art. In essence, he said that all the movements you are making with your body and your thoughts are creating spirals of energy. Your focus is on your hands, your movements, your dance with the energies around you, and on directing them with your intention. When someone comes in to attack you, you don't focus on the other person; you focus on your spirals. The other guy just happens to get in the way.

"The really magical things are the ones that happen right in front of you. A lot of the time you keep looking for beauty, but it is already there. And if you look with a bit more intention, you see it."

— Vik Muniz

More and more people who may be perceived as highly sensitive are being born in this world. Observable skills include a child's ability to see, hear, feel, and experience more about something than what others can pick up. Some are telekinetic, have premonitions, or are able to know things that have not been taught yet, yet are absolutely true. With this sensitivity and awareness, it may be more difficult for them to experience their lives in their bodies—they are getting so much information. When I was little, I was told I was too sensitive when intense energy would come my way. I didn't just hear the angry words; I felt them throughout my body, and it was too much for me to handle. My outlet was crying and retreating into my head, trying not to feel. I would choose to be alone a lot. Shutting down was a coping mechanism common to many who are highly sensitive.

One woman I know who helps highly sensitive people in a variety of amazing ways is Ashley Lee, RN, BSN, CCRN. Being highly sensitive herself, she has been able to teach many skills and techniques to both children and their parents so that they might understand each other better and offer support. Ashley Lee is a Medical Intuitive with twenty-seven years of pediatric and newborn critical care. She is one of the country's leading experts on relieving allergy symptoms in infants. Ashley also works with infants, children, adults, and highly sensitive people (HSP) extensively on brain and nervous system sensory integration. Please visit her website, www.ashleyleehealing.com, for more information. I will begin with a story from her childhood to share an example of an experience a highly sensitive person might have.

Three-year-old Ashley went into her mother's room and shared what she noticed and experienced about her mother's feelings. Her noticing came from great intuition and awareness, yet her mother was not yet aware of these feelings herself. She became angry over the apparent "too big for your britches" words coming from her little daughter (who actually knew more than she did at that moment). Resentment flared up and a backlash occurred. Ashley was just trying to help. Her mother said, "Stop telling me what my feelings are!" As Ashley was leaving, her mother slapped her on her back and said, "Don't you ever do that again." Ashley shut down, no longer sharing her abilities, or connecting with her mother and others. Her system told her it wasn't safe.

This is how it played out in her various layers. The physical aspect was the brain integrating into the body from the slap on the back. "I will be punished when I speak the truth. I will hold onto their anger." The emotional body said, "It's not okay to be me, to support and help." The spiritual body said, "I promise I'll be good. I'll be better. I'll conform. I'll make it comfortable for you." From that experience on, she was wired to operate in those ways when similar events occurred. What Ashley wished her mother had said instead was, "Thanks for being an amazing three year old and supporting me. I'll work on it and it will be okay." What great things can occur when we can acknowledge our child's gifts and keep our egos in check.

I talked with Ashley about her amazing intuitive healing work with HSP, and how we can open the door to greater acknowledging, appreciation, and communication of an HSP's skills and ways of being in the world. Following is some of our conversation.

Meredith: How do you describe HSP? What are the main triggers that can overwhelm them, cause them anxiety, or make them feel disrupted?

Ashley: I feel HSP were born with the gifts of intuitiveness and open energy flow. We are all open vessels, and every human is born with certain special gifts. Everyone, prior to incarnation, has these gifts and is here to explore and expand on them. On a collective level, we all choose our roles to create a particular collective experience.

When a child experiences a negative response to those abilities, judgment or fear from others, the child shuts down. When we shut down, we end up moving into coping. We become hyper-vigilant so no one sees us or knows us. When children and other HSP are comfortable among non-HSP, when they feel safe and loved, they will be able to open up their selves, their abilities, and even gain more highly sensitive skills. Sometimes, people don't want to live in their truth because they have coped for so long that they believe coping is what has made them strong. So to lose the coping mechanism would be to lose their highly sensitive strength.

Meredith: When you work with highly sensitive people, what is the one thing you notice that can most easily be fixed, healed, or managed by themselves?

Ashley: When I work with a client, I ask her or him to get centered and lose the attachment to the outcome—just discern what you are experiencing. Is that yours? Did you feel it because you have a connection to it, something that happened in your own life, or that you wanted to add a resource to help? There are layers that keep our experience stuck in the hyper-vigilant state. The physical body holds the experience through cellular memory. The mental body makes the decision on future behaviors for similar situations. The emotional body holds the emotional imprint or effect such as fear or sadness. The spiritual body will hold onto the resulting belief such as, "I'm not

227

good enough. I don't deserve it." What results is employing coping mechanisms in order to adapt to social norms.

If you walk by a person who is dealing with pain in a grocery store, as a physical empath, you feel the pain in your body. That person didn't ask for help, but you want to offer support. I say to my clients, "Let that person have their feelings. You never took it away from them in the first place. Those are their feelings, but emotional energy is infinite. Consciously imagine giving them back their feelings. Let those emotions out of your body. Since you don't know that person, all you have to do is let the universe rain down all the resources and support needed in the way it is needed in that moment."

For an Acquaintance: Kids don't know how to offer support. They are more direct and abrupt. They process quickly and feel "this needs fixing." Say to the one you feel needs help, "I can feel you might be feeling this way.... Can I offer support…?" in a gentle and compassionate way without being off the Richter scale in an HSP way.

For a Loved One: We can give time, money, or delegate to others to support their wellbeing through emotional or energy support.

Meredith: What can you share with those who care for the highly sensitive child or significant other that would assist in their experiencing the world?

Ashley: Know that it's okay and safe to be an HSP, and actually, it's necessary! I can share *my heart* with others without it being harmful to others. We can use our skills in supportive, positive ways. Use strategies and tools rather than using coping skills—coping skills are really a way of hiding because we don't want to be seen as different.

We want to belong in our biological family and community and feel safe and loved doing so. When we stand in our power, we can enjoy our skills and share them, support others, let others have their experience, and let things go so our bodies are clean and clear for ourselves. Do whatever is appropriate with your social connection to a given person. The goal is to love and support, not to fix. When we can do that, we have moved out of feeling overwhelmed and into greater balance with ourselves and those around us.

"At times you have to leave the city of your comfort and go into the wilderness of your intuition. What you'll discover will be wonderful. What you'll discover is yourself."

— Alan Alda

Othala Rune (O; Ancestral Property). This symbol represents inherited property or possessions, spiritual heritage, experience, and fundamental values. It is viewed as a source of safety, increase, and abundance.

CHAPTER 13

LETTING LOVE FLOW PROPERLY

"I am the living branch of an ancient tree
that is thousands of years old."

— Author Unknown

There is a lot in this world that few people know about, let alone understand or experience. Because of my intuition and premonitions, I was perhaps more curious than most to go down the rabbit hole. Now I help others with similar predicaments. What I found held volumes of answers to my questions, and it helped me heal more deeply than pills or making more friends could have. I wanted to get past this pain part that was stuck and be happier. I was desperate to do so, and in that desperation and seeking, Huna and Family Soul Constellations fell into my lap. Thank you, universe!

We'll talk about Huna in the next chapter, so for now, let me just give you a brief explanation about what Family Soul Constellations is.

The discovery of Family Soul Constellation work rocked my world and opened up so many possibilities for my growth and change. I find that not only is it important to find our physical health balance, but also our emotional balance, too. Because many of our emotions are tied to our childhood, they are also tied to inherited stuck family energy that has not been cleared or released. And these are extremely important elements of our experience and need tending to. Here's why: without cleaning up our childhood, our connections to our family's stuck energy, and our soul's past, we can't shift completely. There are still hanging chads out there, stuck in the past, trying to create resolution for some other family member, just waiting to be healed. We have to gather them up so we can become whole and fully present in our own experience. If we don't, we are doomed to keep that energy around and repeat it—unfortunately at great cost to us. Family Soul Constellation's work addresses love and relationships, money and career, health and wellbeing, and a host of other topics. The bottom line of this soul-based work is to achieve greater "Orders of Love in the Family System and within the Client."

As I shared in Chapter 4, the science world has recently discovered that family memories can be transported through our DNA, but Bert Hellinger, a psychotherapist in Germany, started working with family stuck energy many years ago. It all began when he was working with a female client and came to an impasse. To help move the session along, he stepped into the role of the client's father in a role-playing exercise. As he did so, he surprisingly started feeling not quite himself. He was able to access personality, feelings, and phrases akin to her father's.

After conversing for a while, Hellinger started to see where the family entanglements were. Once entanglements were addressed and love was put properly in its place, with all parties taking responsibility and making amends, love started to flow more freely. Hellinger continued his work, noting repeated patterns of family entanglements and finding effective solutions to restore balance. Once the love was properly restored in the session, love soon became restored in the family in the real world. He learned the nature of the holographic universe. Now we call his work Family Soul Constellation Therapy.

Before we go any further, please review the next set of questions, and notice what you say yes to.

Love:

How well is Love working in your life, in your parents, children, or grandchildren's lives?

Do you want your grandchildren entangled with your failed relationship(s)?

Are you unconsciously trying to leave your parents' marriage because Mom (or Dad) couldn't find the courage to do so?

Are you still replicating your mom's suffering by attracting (or marrying) men who do to you what men did to her? Are you holding yourself distant from the one you love? Are you taking out your anger on your spouse or partner?

How many times have you been divorced? Have you ever been cheated on?

Relationships:

Do you have a hard time making friends? Do you piss people off routinely? Do people not warm up to you? Do you have a hard time being trusted? Do people take out their feelings on you? Do you feel like the scapegoat in your family? Do people blame you for their problems?

Are you always paying for your friends? Do your friends take advantage of you?

Do you get along with your siblings? Is anyone in your family not speaking with you?

Money:

How are you losing the family fortune? Are you letting money slip through your hands? Do you not give a damn about money? Have you ever not had enough to cover the bills? How many times have you lost everything? Do you make a little extra only to have an unexpected bill take it away?

Are you unhappy in your job? Do you love your job but it doesn't pay well?

Do you feel money is bad?

Do you feel you have nothing to show for your money? Do your projects never get off the ground?

Career:

How many times have you been passed over for promotion? How many times have you not been paid equal pay for equal work? Do you make waves at work and then have to leave? Do your colleagues trust you?

Are you changing jobs frequently? Have you not settled on what career you want to be in?

Are people jealous of you at work?

Do you work for companies that fail?

Health:

Do you live with symptoms day in and day out? Do you have unexplained health issues? How many near-death experiences have you had?

Do you suffer from something other relatives have suffered from? Do you believe you are going to suffer the same death as others in your family?

While we are on the subject of what is driving your suffering, let me ask you a favorite question of mine: What sucks the most for you?

Your answer will almost inevitably point to your entanglement with someone in your family.

"But wait!" you might say. "I don't remember making a decision to suffer!" And you would be right. These decisions were made on the soul level between conception and age seven. Age seven is when reason and logic begin to dominate our experiences. In general, we are not very creative people. Our souls have a strong desire to show love and loyalty to those we hope to help. We replicate their pain and suffering in an unworkable attempt to fix it. The magical thinking of the young soul is what got you and others into what sucks the most.

For example, to illustrate the magical thinking connected to a young child's entanglement, consider a scenario whereby a young boy hears his father come home each night when the bars close and then he hears his mother getting beaten; his mother threatens to leave his father if he doesn't stop beating her. The young child makes an unconscious decision to help save his parents and their marriage. The internal dialog goes something like this: "Dear Father, in your honor, I will drink so you don't have to. If you don't have to, you won't get drunk. If you aren't drunk, you won't beat Mom, and then Mom won't threaten to leave us. If she doesn't leave us, I will feel safe, happy, and loved." Meanwhile, the child starts to drink to become the alcoholic that Dad has become, and even though Mom has already left, he keeps drinking until eventually he dies driving under the influence at a very young age. This didn't solve anything. And more importantly, he never survived to see the *intended positive outcome* his drinking was to have in fixing his parents.

Another example is Maya Angelou. At age seven and a half, she was raped and sent to the hospital for care. The rapist was well known to the family, so once he was released from jail, he was dead the next day, kicked to death. Because she had spoken his name, she felt directly responsible for his death, so she chose not to speak for five years. She read every book in the library instead. Her magical thinking made her act in a certain way to solve her dilemma.

Intended positive outcomes (IPOs) are the key to Entanglements. Sometimes unintended consequences happen to our IPOs. Here's an example: A woman has a new boss who is just awful to work with. Every morning, she has bad feelings about knowing who she has to face that day. In the morning on the way to work, she stops to buy a coffee. To assuage her bad feelings, she also buys a sugar donut or two and eats them before getting into the office. The "treats" were to make her feel better, which they did for a few minutes. But twelve months of sugar binging in the morning to face work and twenty unwanted pounds later, her IPO had some significant unintended consequences.

What is the *hidden force* here? Is it really the sugar in the donuts? Is it really the boss? No. A deeper look might reveal that her own obese father was subject to many years of abuse by a bad boss but felt powerless in a weak economy with five mouths to feed. Family Constellations helps stop the painful patterns by offering a re-solution to the soul of the one *entangled* and the ones who are suffering upstream in the family tree.

Here is how it works: In a session, the facilitator will sit down with the client and ask about what the client wants as an outcome (an area to focus) and then ask about family history. What is the current unwanted experience, and what occurred in the past? What major riffs occurred that broke families apart or caused great pain? What traumas occurred, such as suicide, untimely deaths, miscarriages, sudden loss in wealth, relocation, separation, disabilities, etc. Once the family is understood, the facilitator will know where to look in the family history for the solution to the current predicament. It has been my experience that what needs to show up will always show up. Even if there was an unknown, never discussed event that happened long ago and far away, it can be found by applying this method. It works in an uncanny way finding what is needed to heal the client.

Before we go any further, I need to share a leap that might be useful for understanding how this whole process works. The universe and you are connected in the sense that we can get information at any time when we focus on it. Kinesiology is possible because of this fact.

Shamans have learned to do this, and intuitives and highly sensitive people are naturally attuned to be able to do it. We are like little radio towers tuning into all the information across space and time, which is passing through us all the time. We just have to learn how to tune our instruments to receive the information.

A constellation will continue like this: The facilitator will write on some cards, fold them up, shuffle them, and then ask the client either to place them on the floor where that person feels they need to go, or give them to people who offer to represent whatever is written on the card. The client will give each representative a folded card and move the representative around the open room where the client sees fit. They always seem to go just in the right spot somehow and make sense when the great reveal later occurs. With blank minds and without any information on the client's history, the representatives are blank slates and get a very clean "download" of the energy/information that needs to come through for the client. No one knows what the cards are except for the facilitator, but once the cards are shuffled, the session becomes double blind. No one knows anything about what is about to happen, or what will be uncovered and set free.

A client, Patti, came to me frustrated because she hadn't been in a relationship for a long while. Her ex-husband was a very intense individual; he was also very shifty and would pull the rug out from under her with his lies. All of her past relationships were like this—she even had people who wanted to be her partner but she just thought of as friends. She seemed to be a magnet for this dynamic! We needed to have her stop scanning for this scenario, and we needed to get to the imprint. So I asked her when she first experienced this situation, long ago and far away. I told her, using specific NLP language, "Grow yourself younger and just put a tag on all those experiences when that feeling and experience occurred." She did. We went back into the past, so far in fact, that we popped out of her life and into her great-great-great-grandmother, who was horribly lied to by her husband, which caused a schism in the family for generations. Wow! My client was unconsciously replicating this experience in her own life to point it out to her family and help them fix the past in the present. She had never met her ancestor, but in an unworkable attempt to say "I love you," she picked up this scenario energetically in her own life. As you may have already noticed, not only was her love life a mess, but it still wasn't fixing the past as she had hoped.

If you haven't experienced a constellation before, I would not be surprised if you were quite skeptical. I hear you and understand the incredulity and even cynicism, but you have stuck with me so far, so let's keep going a little further! I used to feel that way, too, until I kept going to Constellation sessions and found re-emerging patterns and resolutions occur every time. The healing was not only happening for the client, but the family is shifted as well—without even knowing the Constellation session occurred. I have learned that the client's mother's chronic pain was soon eliminated without the mother even knowing the constellation occurred. The constellation showed the mother's father literally standing on the mother's neck trying to crush her spirit into the ground. The leg pain was a result of her trying to stand on her own and be in her own power. Now she could. This really worked!

The double-blind process in the constellation removes preconceived notions and keeps everyone extremely clean. Over and over and over again, with different clients, circumstances, family history, and so forth, patterns emerge every single time when love was denied, responsibility was rejected, great sadness and death occurred; it always showed up. And when it was seen and acknowledged, the room's energy would finally shift and rather than feeling tense, a lightness started to come into the room. The locations of people in the room started to move. People were starting to stand in their truth and carry their weight and responsibility. Truly awesome.

When the energy is not flowing well or at all, we ask as facilitators, "What needs to happen to make love flow properly?" What needs to happen if people stand in the truth of what has occurred and take responsibility for themselves and their part in the family appropriately? Once that is done, the pain in the client—whether it is manifested as physical or emotional, as addictions or anger, an inability to stay in a relationship or a job, etc.—gets relief. The client is then able to live his or her life for just him- or herself and not for the pain of the family. The client's suffering obligation of love has been reassigned to more fruitful pursuits.

How does the sadness from a few generations back manifest in the here and now? Recently, I had a client who, quite literally, was shouldering a burden for her ex-husband's pain. The constellation showed a person on the floor looking away from the "root cause" card. The client's representative was in the middle of the room with great shoulder pain, kneeling on the floor in agony. "What would make your pain better?" The representative asked, pointing to the "root case" card on the floor, "If that one on the floor got up and took care of it." Okay, we were starting to understand what was needed to have love and responsibility rightfully placed. We had the person on the floor stand up, even though that one didn't want to, and look at the "root cause." Then I, the facilitator, suggested that the person say to the client's representative while pointing to the root cause, "That's mine. I own that." Instantly, the client's representative felt relief. She could get off the floor, and her shoulders and back did not hurt anymore. I occasionally check in with the client and so far, so good. It has only been a few weeks, but I look forward to seeing how this constellation has helped shift her experience.

Mental health always has underlying issues of emotional and/or spiritual components. What part of your body found it useful to store a disease until it was time to use it to get your attention? Quantum physics is showing us that the body is not solid, but a constant collision of particles and electrons. Emotions and thoughts are also just energy, and the lower the frequency, the denser the body. With all those energies flowing through the body, it is no wonder that a disturbance in one layer directly affects the others and continues rippling through the body until the disturbance is released.

What we have found in the past with Family Constellations is that schizophrenia occurs because the client is trying to heal the stuck relationship (from long ago and far away in the family tree) between the victim and perpetrator within himself. The victim and perpetrator both have a rightful place in the family system, even if one is outside the family tree. In some rare cases, entanglements with two very diverse people who may or may not be attached can create warring factors inside the person's mind. This is only one example of how we can use the family constellation format for health updates to the body.

Another example concerns autism. My colleague and fellow practitioner, Anne Marie Peterson-Kolatkar, and I helped an autistic boy who was unfortunately quite disruptive in class. He would scream and yell often, and no one could really figure out how to stop this behavior.

He wasn't trying to cause a scene, but something was going on that was causing this experience to occur. When Annie and I checked in with his experience through the Family Constellation format, he was covering his ears and just getting overloaded with information from the tangible world and also the unseen world. His system was so sensitive that he was picking up on tons of information that the average human does not experience. What did we do? We cleared out a lot of those people giving the information, and we asked the benevolent ones to dial their information down and maybe even talk one at a time. Problem solved! The next day in class, he did not scream once, and that has continued, except for the occasional yell from being startled by another, but even those yells are nowhere near the intensity he previously showed. We are so glad he is doing better.

A colleague of mine, Michael J. Peterson, figured out that the constellation format could be used for other things like clearing entities and energies from people and spaces. He noted that his clients were getting deeper insights and consequently bigger shifts. As he likes to say, "I help people identify the feelings that are theirs, the feelings that are not theirs, and then turn off the feelings that are not theirs."

In an interview, Anne Marie Peterson-Kolatkar compared life with attached entities as "living under a glass dome." She explains it like this:

> Imagine living under a glass dome with all the bad feelings trapped inside with you. Everywhere you go, they are there with you. No matter how many times you put your credit card up to the glass to pay for therapy, take a meditation or yoga class, buy carbs, drugs, or alcohol, etc., you only get temporary relief. And soon the old feelings come back. Nothing changes. Why? Because entities are holding in your

negative experiences and you are feeling stuck. The non-resourceful part of this is that your brain is constantly checking in on those negative feelings to see whether you are surviving them. When a clearing is complete, the proverbial glass dome is lifted, and good things start to happen. A person is free to be their sovereign self.

She noted that she won't begin doing family constellation work until each client she sees is cleared of these entities and negative energies—that is how much impact it has for the individual.

Exercise

Write down your family history of events or dynamics that catch your attention.

_____

_____

_____

_____

_____

_____

_____

_____

_____

_____

_____

_____

_____

What actions are you prepared to take to help resolve these issues in your family, and most of all, to find peace within yourself?

_____

_____

_____

_____

_____

_____

_____

"To enjoy good health, to bring true happiness to one's family, to bring peace to all, one must first discipline and control one's own mind. If a man can control his mind he can find the way to Enlightenment, and all wisdom and virtue will naturally come to him."

— Buddha

This Tibetan endless knot symbol reminds us how all phenomena are conjoined and yoked together as a closed cycle of cause and effect.

CHAPTER 14

HEALING WITH HUNA

"When the body is in trouble, we must find and eliminate the cause, not medicate the symptom."

— Nina Leavins

I lay there on the floor with my eyes closed and felt a weight as heavy as a bowling ball on my stomach. We had just started journeying in our Huna class, where the client closes his or her eyes and is guided into a relaxed state. Once the client is relaxed, the session begins, but for me, before anything actually started, there was the weight of a bowling ball on my stomach. I peeked open my right eye to see who had his or her hand on me, but not one hand or arm or body part was anywhere near me. Odd. "Okay, guys," I said, "I'm feeling a weight on my stomach here. What is happening?" "It's not me; I'm just sitting here," said my neighbor. And thus began my introduction into the wonderful world of Huna (Hawaiian Spirituality) where unseen forces are brought to light and uncovered as being part of your human experience.

Hawaiians look at illness and troubles in a very different way than how Western medicine does. If, for example, a child breaks her leg, the people ask, "Why did you break your leg?" You might think that very strange, but it is the perspective that we are not victims of circumstance in our experience, but that we are co-creators of our worlds. There is an interplay with all things and Huna is a gentle way of getting to the root cause of the trouble—then setting it free. Once in a hypnotic state, one can travel to any point in time in one's experience to see what's what. Sometimes, what you uncover is not quite what you expected but very useful all the same.

I closed my eyes again, trusting the process. We are just talking, and I have my eyes closed. *Simple enough, I suppose,* I thought. *I am just going to be asked questions, right? How weird could that be?* Well, my naïve little self was in for a ride. I came into the session wanting to know why I always felt like a weight was on me, and so I drilled down to figure out what was going on. Down the rabbit hole we went—talking to the subconscious. The good thing about the subconscious is that it never lies, and once in a relaxed state, you can access it more easily because your guard is down. It's fairly easy to do so because you know you are in a trusted, safe environment with respectable people, and the facilitator asks very clear, concise, non-leading questions.

So, I had my goal already set and there was this bowling ball feeling on my stomach. "Okay, weight on my belly, what can I call you?" asks the facilitator. Morris came to mind. It was male, and very, very big. An image came to me; it looked like a very large bear. Uh, what? Perhaps it's a metaphor. I'll go with it, sure. Now I have had visions before, but this was bizarre. As the session progressed, I learned that the soul of this bear felt my sadness when I was very little and came to help—to ease my sadness and be my protector. He came to help and remained with me until that moment. I had a choice to make.

When we learn the story of how and why an entity came to be with us, there is always a choice to be made. Most often the client will choose to have the entity or entities leave because they bring their own baggage with them, and the person just wants to have his or her own experience, which makes sense. Some baggage I have witnessed with entities are memories, physical pains taken from previous deaths, addictions, fears, and more. Even though there may be more than one soul occupying a body, the body responds to *all* the input it is receiving.

Some beings are just not nice and *are* there to harm you. Those require a deft hand for imposing very clear rules. When push comes to shove, I call for help, and help comes from above—from beings who have a lot more power and ability than I currently have learned to access. Light has literally filled the room on occasion, sending harmful beings away. What is surprising, however, is that often those who have come to do harm end up being just very angry or scared individuals who were taken advantage of and disillusioned by bigger and darker forces. But all beings have a choice, and when given the choice, they often will go to the light side with much relief.

Entities

How does this happen anyway, this conjoining of beings? I have experienced that it happens when a trauma, sadness, or stress creates a hole in the person's auric field. With that opening, others might want to fill it, to help, or to feed off of the person's energy. Or there is an energetic match. Both beings are feeling the same way and whoosh! The Law of Attraction pulls them together almost instantaneously. Look, I never knew this existed, either. I grew up Christian, imagining you got one shot, one life, and if you were good, you went to heaven; if you were bad, you went to hell. Case closed. But, apparently, the world is a little more complex than that. Let me go through some of what I know so you can understand more of this.

Cardinal Rule: One Body, One Soul

The cardinal rule of the universe is that a body is allowed, ultimately, only one soul. Should you find that there is more than one soul occupying that space, well, the original soul has the right to kick everybody out. Gives you a new appreciation of rights against squatters, huh? It is actually quite easy to do (most of the time), but it does require awareness, clarity, and proper intention. Most sessions have fairly gentle and happy outcomes. Often the beings who came to help accidentally got stuck in the process. Toward the end of the session, there is a meeting of the minds, reconciliation, and a sharing of final wishes of knowledge and understanding between all involved. Then the earthbound spirit will go back to where it came from, go to the light, or go wherever it feels the next place to go is. Often I guide them, especially when there is confusion about them being dead at all.

On this planet, billions of people, animals, and other souls cycle through their lives, and when the body is no more, their souls actually do go somewhere. Some transition into the light, some stay to help family or friends, some stay because they don't know they are dead, some stay because they are angry that something didn't work out, and some are so fearful that they just don't know *where* to go and don't ask anyone for help. These non-passed-over beings sometimes cruise around; some look for help and some attach to others. For those who do need help to transition, I will help them in any way I can—I step aside from what I am doing, wherever I am, when I feel them, and then I guide them to the appropriate place.

Those who have had sessions with me have been extremely surprised by the root causes of their predicaments. I have had people with recurring nightmares, chronic pains, addictions, and weird experiences who have tried everything to fix the problem. Sometimes with pain or addiction, it's not Western medicine you need but a deeper look into the soul to notice what is really being held, how and why, so you can become able to let it go.

Light/Dark

The light is filled with higher, more refined vibrations than here on the earthly plane. I have come into contact with angels, guides, masters, and many others. But it is subtle and sometimes difficult to track because, well, we are used to being in a more fearful state. Imagine being extraordinarily happy all day long without one fear popping up. Right. Now, imagine being angry and fearful all day without any lightness or happiness occurring. The feeling is heavier, darker, thicker. The experiences are very different.

When one is in a more fearful and stressed state, or sick, one can open up to those who will prey on that feeling. One might hear voices, or subtle notions that don't quite seem like self, but are so very close to what one might already believe that one may believe it is one's own thoughts. And on it can go until one is, over time, in a very dark place, emotionally and perhaps physically. Evil, dark forces do exist, and they will use lots of trickery to get you to do what they want. They will use your energy, they will confuse you, they can interfere with your relationships, and they can amplify the negative feelings you have toward a person. I, personally, had an entity sabotaging my relationship with my husband. I didn't catch it for a long time, until it got so bad I asked for help from a friend. Instantly, my relationship with my husband was more calm and open. We still had to own our parts in the relationship, but the dynamics shifted to a much calmer state.

A friend, April, once told me about how she, a Catholic, had experienced this strong voice inside her head one afternoon in her home. It was willing her to throw her child out the window. It scared her to death because she never had a notion until that moment to do anything like that. No, it was not postpartum depression or anything like schizophrenia. The voice in her head didn't sound like her nor feel like her. It baffled her. She felt a battle of wills until she literally forced it, whatever or whoever it was, out of her space with her will and prayer. She never understood nor truly believed in these forces until that experience.

When I was introduced to what the dark forces were and what they could do, I was completely horrified and scared out of my mind. Thoughts of *The Exorcist* would rattle my mind. However, once I became more comfortable with the work, more confident in my expanding skills, and really understood who I was, I could see the subtle shifts and then check in to see whether it was just me being tired or off emotionally due to stress, or whether it was someone hacking my experience. If the red flag went up, I cleared them out. I check in every day and clear it out. I have my routine. Stillness, ground, shield, clear, stillness, ground, stay in my center, breathe deeply, and then go about my day.

A Simple Clearing

Say this in your head or out loud. It doesn't matter. It just matters that you declare what you want.

Say: "Let's clear all entities attached and non-attached, negatively influencing me and my relationships across space and time. Let's go ahead and clear the first group now." And go on with each group until you feel you are done. The more practice you get, the more you will be able to feel the subtle differences in your experience before and after the clearing.

During this, you can use what is called a pendulum (a short chain with a weight on the end) to see when you are done if you are not familiar with the feeling of "being done." The pendulum is simply a way for you to notice what movements your body is already doing. When you are clearing, your body will tend to move, and you might notice the pendulum swinging or spinning in a certain direction—that movement will stop when you are cleared.

When you are done, then you balance yourself, filling up all the holes with white light or your highest vibration. Check in with yourself on how those holes got created in the first place. Where were you out of balance? Be honest; then work on those parts. Check in periodically to notice any shifts and reset yourself accordingly.

Acknowledging Our Body

Do you remember the hiking story where I dislocated my elbow? I had done lots of physical therapy on it, but it was still very tight and painful around the joint. The pain just wouldn't go away, even after trying massages and everything else I knew about. A few months later, I thought my elbow was not going to get better. Then a friend of mine who practiced Huna said she would help me. What did she do? She talked to my elbow. I relaxed on the floor and she talked to it, saying how brave it was and how it did such an amazing job at keeping Meredith safe. She acknowledged what had happened. And then this surprising thing happened. Strings of tension just released instantaneously around my old wound. Like a guitar string being plucked, the muscular tissues just started releasing and relaxing. The muscles didn't need to hold on anymore. Their job was done, and they were relieved of their duty. My brain allowed the muscles to release in a way that massage couldn't, physical therapy couldn't, and stretching couldn't. What other ways could this technique help others? I was determined to find out.

Past Lives

The first book I read about the subject of past lives was *Many Lives, Many Masters* by Brian Weiss, M.D. It exposed me to the possibility that we don't just get one life here and then go to heaven or hell. This psychiatrist used hypnosis in an effort to uncover the imprints from a client's childhood that would explain her phobias and nightmares, but she wasn't turning up anything, so she said, "Let's go back to where it started," essentially. And when she was regressed and looked down at her feet, she found herself in a very different place, a very long time ago. Dr. Weiss followed her and what she was experiencing, even though he didn't quite comprehend what was happening initially. He came to learn after uncovering these stories that her psyche was trapped in horrible memories from previous lives. Once he uncovered the root cause, he was able to do his great work to begin the healing process.

Many documented cases exist of children who have had memories of their past lives. Some are subtle and some are more profound. The most recently circulated story is of a boy, James Leininger, who constantly had nightmares about his plane going down during World War II. "Plane on fire! Little man can't get out!" he would scream. In the book *Soul Survivor: The Reincarnation of a World War II Fighter Pilot*, authors Bruce and Andrea Leininger share the story of their son who had nightmares from early childhood to the age of eight. His parents were frightened at first, then tried to shrug it off, but because of the details he was able to share, they were left with the undeniable truth that their son was this man in his dreams. They got a name and learned that James Huston was a pilot in World War II, flew a Corsair, and was killed in action on the Natoma. Their search took them to James' still living wife and she corroborated the facts.

Helping Them into the Light

A client, Liz, kept having dreams of a white house. It wasn't necessarily a bad dream, but she kept dreaming of this white house. She was interested in my work, and we had a session on New Year's Day a few years ago to see what the dream was about. When I journeyed with her, I saw the grass, an old tractor, and the white house in the middle of the day. I ventured inside and found a scene of great sadness. The whole family was dead, killed by a drifter who escaped from prison in the South. When I journeyed to the basement, I found the father who had died but hadn't gone into the light. He instead remained on this plane, wandering about until he noticed Liz. He noticed something within her and instantaneously became attached—he wanted to help her. After I had a conversation with this man, clearing up any misunderstandings, anger, sadness, and all that kept him here, he was able to leave and go where he needed to go. The memories Liz was experiencing were not her own, but his. When he left, she no longer had the dreams.

A similar experience I had began with a client who had a four-year-old daughter. This little girl was literally scaring people with the intensity of her angry stare, although I thought she was a lovely child, always bright and happy. How on earth could a little child scare someone so much? That sounds a little overly dramatic, I thought, but I've seen some amazing things so anything is possible. Well, I was hanging out with her on one occasion when she disagreed with me on something I was asking her to do. She sent this wave of anger at me so strongly I literally lost my breath and stepped back to rebalance myself. Wow! That's a new one.

I looked at her curiously and noticed something else in her eyes that I knew wasn't all her. There was something or someone that was older, taunting, and menacingly angry. When I went home later, I checked in with who this being was. I settled into stillness and saw in my mind's eye that this person was a gunslinger type of a man from many years before who had once been at a prison in the vicinity and died there. As he was now a free-roaming soul, he decided to join up with this little girl who was emotionally calling out for help. As the youngest child in her family, it seemed she felt she needed some strength to help her. In honor of this girl, I helped the man find his way home and helped her find her own resources and power already within her. She hasn't scared anyone since and is happier than ever.

Ho'o Pono Pono: Making It Right

One of the most beautiful phrases used for clearing and realigning the energies is Ho'o Pono Pono. It means to make it right. It was developed by Morrnah N. Simeona. There are two versions I know and use. The more commonly known is this: I'm sorry. Please forgive me. I thank you. I love you.

All you notice within someone else is also within you. Remember the holographic universe concept? So as you heal within yourself, you are also healing outside of yourself, in all things, to the Divine, to True Source. You are asking for healing for whatever brought what needs to be healed or shifted to you. You are asking for the ability to forgive yourself—you are expressing gratitude and love. That outpouring of amazing expansive transformative energy transmutes what is stuck into flowing positive movement.

Ihaleakala Hew Len, Ph.D., used this prayer to help heal people in a psychiatric ward in Hawaii. I heard he never met his patients. He looked at their files, and with all he could draw upon, inside and outside of himself, he would use this prayer, directing these energies to the patient and to what needed to be healed. Over time, people started to become well and get off their medications. A few years later, the hospital closed down. There were no patients needing its services. This cleaning process and "love in action" can be used for anyone and anything, and the more powerful you are, the more powerful the prayer becomes. It sets the past energies to neutral or zero, a new launching point from which to live.

Have you ever had a small memory, persistent dream, or fear where you just couldn't quite fathom where it came from? Perhaps it's a strong wish to keep your family safe. Maybe you have a phobia that makes no sense. Maybe it's a persistent pain, a birthmark, or even an addiction. Write down below those things that don't make sense.

Exercise

Write down any experiences, behaviors, and/or feelings that you would like to have cleared and set free.

_____

_____

_____

_____

_____

_____

_____

_____

_____

_____

_____

_____

"A peaceful man does more good than a learned one."

— Pope John XXIII

The Triquetra symbol is of Celtic origin. A modern translation is a connection of mind, body, and soul, the three parts overlapping in the middle.

CHAPTER 15

BEING HERE NOW

"A quiet mind is all you need. All else will happen rightly, once your mind is quiet. As the sun on rising makes the world active, so does self-awareness affect changes in the mind. In the light of calm and steady self-awareness, inner energies wake up and work miracles without any effort on your part."

— Nisargadatta Maharaj

Not only do you have the physical, emotional, mental, and spiritual aspects to keep track of, but you have your family soul and entities to clear out and soul fragments to reintegrate so you can finally just be you being you here, now, in all the ways that you are. And while it may be daunting to think about getting all this done, the more you check in with yourself, clear, and align, the easier it will be in the future. There will also be less to do because you will have already done a lot! Soon enough, it will just be maintenance, a few minutes a day to check in.

If you have a lot of things to take care of, start with the one thing that will relieve the most stress. Then choose the next thing. You have a whole lifetime, multiple lifetimes even, to do this! So take one thing at a time. It's not a race. The more obstacles you take down and reconcile, the easier your life will become. It may take a while to believe it's not a fluke, but as you become brighter, stronger, and more aligned, you will notice the world become so, too. The universe is your mirror.

When I was taking singing classes, the best sounds I created were when I stopped trying to push the sound through my chest and let it flow out naturally. The resonance was no longer in my chest or vocal chords, but in my nose. When there was ease, openness, and trust, the resonance was amazing. And effortless. It was so much less work! I used to try to muscle the sound out, so a teacher told me to practice singing upside down. Yes, upside down. For one, it scrambled my brain, and two, it prevented me from having to force anything out—the power versus force conundrum. Power won out and the effects were startling. When one just lets go of what one thinks should be and tries to listen to what the body is trying to say, talents just unfold and appear, as if it is the easiest thing in the world.

"Nothing is worth losing your Peace."

— Baba Harihar Ramji, *Sonoma Ashram*

I am reminded of the movie *Kung Fu Panda*, where Panda, after months of training, fighting, and breaking through barriers and obstacles, finally finds the scroll he has been fighting for. He slowly unrolls the scroll that is supposed to be the key to enlightenment and the end of suffering. As he opens it, he is faced with a mirror—a perfect reflection of himself. Not just his image but what he sees, and truly what he believes about himself and the world. He smiles in awe and then understanding. He is the key to his own enlightenment. Only he has the tools and the wisdom to become enlightened, but only after doing his homework: fighting the demons of illusion his ego has created. The illusions keep us separated from our highest selves, from being able to greet each obstacle with greater balance and peace.

When you watch yourself unfold, stop trying to keep ego on top, and keep everything in its place, you no longer struggle with the past or become anxious about your future. You have arrived at now, and it is the only place you want to be. Resistance is replaced with wonder. Frustration and judgment are replaced with compassion. Fear is replaced with love. Time is replaced with now. Struggle to control everything is replaced with consent to what will come, as it does, in all the right ways. There is great beauty in all of that.

I am not saying that once you face higher levels of truth, there will never be sadness nor frustration (the ego keeps on keeping on!), but you will have the tools to move through it more quickly and move higher still, refining more, if that is where you want to go. If you do, then you are able to see the next obstacle more objectively, be less attached to it, understand that it is a tool for you to experience a lesson, experience whatever reason it is there, and then grow and expand. Each layer of letting go will bring more peace and a further refinement to your vibration and your perspective.

"No man ever steps in the same river twice,
for it's not the same river and he's not the same man."

— Heraclitus

263

A lecture about a river by a Sufi teacher shifted my awareness about what "being" really meant. We are human "beings." Animals, rocks, trees, and beyond are "being," but I used to think of them more as being in a stagnant form, as non-changing things. I used to think a river was a river was a river. But this Sufi teacher described a river as more than just water flowing downhill. It is also its banks that hold it in place. It is also the soil and stone beneath keeping it flowing. And what's more, the river is never the same in the same place for more than one moment. I began to ask after that lecture, "Is our being nothing more than an awareness or a continuous stream of experiencing consciousness?" Buckminster Fuller explained this idea of pattern integrity in *Tunings* using two connected ropes, one manila and the other nylon. He tied a knot and massaged it along the path of one rope and massaged it onto the other until the end, where the knot disappeared.

"So I see that the knot was not the rope.
It was the rope that made it possible for you and I to see it,
to tune it in. But it was not the rope....

I see you and I as a sort of complex of slipknots
sliding along on pure principal."

— Buckminster Fuller

Enjoying the Moment

When I spent summers in Montana as a teenager, we would go on a cattle drive at the beginning of July, bringing the cattle up to Bureau of Land Management land in the mountains. Even though the drive was only one day long, our family and friends would all gather for a fun week of fishing, riding horses, cooking, playing pool, watching fireworks on Independence Day, and watching thunderstorms. The thunderstorms were my favorite part. The heat of the day would create these massive thunderheads that would move quickly over the land. A huge cloud that looked a mile across would be there one minute and gone a few minutes later. The storms were dynamic, loud, and the bright flashes and streaks of light lit the night sky. The storms fizzled out by midnight because there was no more heat to create the updrafts and the drama. These storms were always a highlight of my summer.

During one particular year, our group of about fifteen people were on the porch having a late lunch. Really dark, ominous clouds were barely visible over the southern horizon, slowly moving east. The storm was miles away, but we really hoped for it to come. We knew dark clouds moving slowly meant a storm with a lot of power—and the more power, the more I enjoyed the storm. For about an hour, we watched the cloud move slowly and willed it to come north to us. We were itching for a good storm. It ended up being the best one I have ever experienced. We were not thinking about anything else; we were fully present during the whole experience.

Many of our friends left to read or relax elsewhere, but my dad and I kept watching it, asking it to come. It changed direction in the late afternoon and started moving our way. We were shocked and very hopeful. This was too good to be true. By about six o'clock, it was getting closer, and the sky was slowly getting darker, but it wasn't there yet. The storm was building and building, and the tension of anticipation was ever-increasing in our house. We watched the lightning light up the clouds and occasionally strike the ground miles away. By about ten o'clock, it was a few miles away, and by eleven, it was right overhead, booming and hailing all around us, with big strikes less than a mile away. And we saw it all. We were at the epicenter of the storm, in a house in the middle of the valley. It didn't get any better than that!

Bearing Witness to Your Body

Giving birth to my daughter was an amazing experience I will never forget. I was really set on not taking drugs because their potential results scared me off. I would not accept any unless I absolutely had to. I wanted to be present and have my child be present, too. I wanted my body to do what it needed to do, and if it could, then I would go along for the ride. I supposed that women had been doing it for millennia, so surely I could, too. It was all a noble concept, initially, until the first contraction hit. Then I became extremely scared and contracted mentally and physically. Realizing this, I had to practice what I had learned from my hypnobirthing classes—breathe deeply and access all the wisdom I can. I started to listen to the wisdom that was already there, that was carried in my DNA from all the mothers before me. I moved and rolled my hips, lay in the water, and just turned my brain off the best I could. It wasn't needed right now. Besides, my brain didn't know what sense to make of all these extremely intense sensations. I also had a glass of wine. I figured that since we got this far, a little assistance to mellow me a bit would, in the scheme of things, be all right. My husband and doula kept me calm and focused on that moment—not thirty seconds from now, not two seconds from now, but now as it was, and it helped immensely.

Fear takes us out of the present, tenses our bodies up, and sends us on a crazy wild ride all over the universe of possibilities so that we can then try to "control" our situation and make our next move. We are not in reality, but in the realm of possibilities. To stay present and in the moment requires leaps of faith until you realize, through study and intention, that there is nothing to fear. You are doing the best you can. They are doing the best they can. We are all in this amazing ride called life together. When we get beyond judgments, fears, lack, anything that contracts the soul, there is nothing but peace.

"The bad news is you're falling through the air, nothing to hang on to, no parachute. The good news is there's no ground."

— Chogyam Trungpa

The body kept doing what it did and I couldn't really do a thing to change it. The birth was happening on its own, and I was just there for the ride. What an interesting and new experience. When you have learned to meet more and more experiences with clarity, calm, you realize you already *are* clarity, you already *are* calm. You and it are the same. There is no separation and no thinking that it could be anything else. The ego serves its purpose, keeping you alive and safe, and now there is understanding that the ego is not you. It can take a backseat and be used appropriately. That competition has kept you striving to beat the other person, to come out on top of whatever mountain you were climbing. Fear, ego's guard, has kept you safe and allowed you to find connection with "others," and now you know that it is "in here."

Your connecting positively to others—teachers, bosses, family, friends, strangers, animals—all taught you to trust and share.

Connecting with the World

When one is more actively conscious and connected with the world, amazing things can happen. One day I found a beautiful blue polished rock on the rough granite gravel path after facilitating a constellation. Having never seen it before during my weeding expeditions, it stuck out. Perhaps a bird dropped it, I thought, but it didn't feel true. The rock, coincidentally, was beneath the very spot where I held my client's hand to help her down the stairs. I even called my client to see whether she had dropped a stone from her pocket or jewelry. She said that she didn't bring anything with her. When I asked another friend about this weird coincidence, she told me she'd had a similar experience. She told me the rock was a gift from the universe to help me on my path. When I picked up the rock, a headache slowly came on. I put it down a few minutes later, and my headache went away. This rock had a lot of energy. Everyone who has held it has the same response (even if I don't tell them the effects it has on me). After some research online, I learned that this stone was sodalite, which apparently, according to http://www.healing-crystals-for-you.com:

> will bring your attention to the qualities of idealism and truth. It has strong metaphysical properties that may stimulate latent creative abilities and it aids teachers, writers, and students in understanding deeper philosophical principles. Its energy is particularly helpful to aid the development of psychic abilities and with developing intuition. It is an excellent aid to communication

and may help you if you are speaking publicly.

Perhaps it was all just coincidence, but it is interesting that the stone came to me right after a very important constellation, during the beginning stages of writing this book, and the launch of my new career. But of course, it could just be a rock that just happened to land there by accident.

On one trip to Hawaii, our Huna teacher gifted us a few late night initiations. In the quietest of hours, we silently wandered certain locations to learn, to sense, and to open up our intuition further. On one particular night at 3 a.m., I was walking down a path when I saw a beautiful blue light emanating from a wall. It was not a streetlight. To be clear, there was no electricity for half a mile or more, but a soft blue light was coming out in a spherical shape. I instantly knew the origin of the light and its purpose: What was placed in the wall was to create safety and security for what the wall was surrounding and holding sacred. Just like some people in olden times had superstitions that made them keep coins or shoes to protect their homes, so I believe that whatever was in this wall was doing the same. I scoured the Internet. I came up with nothing. I searched and searched, but I came up empty-handed. I suppose I never needed the Internet to tell me what I already knew, but the ego wanted proof that what I saw was real. I had never seen anything before like that light, but I marveled at the idea of all that is just beyond most people's awareness. There are some that have this gift, and see energy come from all things, some more powerful than others. This experience not only taught me that there is more to the universe than I ever knew, but that there is energy flowing in all things. If we pay attention, we will begin to notice it and have a greater dialogue with it.

A man I knew by the name of Marcus was having a bad day quite a few years ago and leaned against a tree to take some time out and sit and think, mumbling to himself about how frustrated he was. Soon enough, he actually heard the tree literally talk back to him. He was *shocked!* He looked around and didn't see anyone around. No human was nearby. He soon enough realized that he was hearing the tree have a conversation with him. "Well, you think *you're* having a bad day! Let me tell you what I have to deal with…." What a surprise he had that day!

I Am That

Every being is alive and connected to every other being, it seems, and more than that, everything has a consciousness, too. Cleve Backster, a world-renowned CIA polygrapher in the 1960s wrote a book documenting his work called *Primary Perception: Biocommunication with Plants, Living Foods, and Human Cells*. He hooked up a plant to the polygraph and then thought about harming the plant. The plant, surprisingly, reacted as evidenced by the needle on the polygraph starting to jump all over the place. When he stopped thinking about causing harm, the needle switched to a calmer rhythm. He did this type of experiment with all sorts of things—eggs, cells, and more. His conclusion was that there is energy and connection between more things than we think. Plants also react when we focus our mind or consciousness on them.

So, if other beings react to our consciousness, why can't our bodies react to our conscious thought, as well?

"Don't worry if you feel you can only do one tiny good thing in one small corner of the cosmos. Just be a Buddha body in that one place."

— Thich Nhat Han

The Infinity symbol represents a potential infinity. It has had a long history in mathematics and is often thought to be a variant form of the Roman numeral for 1,000 or the Greek letter Ω (omega). It was also used to mean "many." In 1655, John Wallis was credited for this symbol, which he wrote in his *De sectionibus conicis*. In modern symbolism, it has been identified with ouroboros, which is seen at the head of Chapter 4, or even Mobius strip, which is described as "a surface with only one side and only one boundary."

CHAPTER 16

WAKING UP

"By prevailing over all obstacles and distractions,
one may unfailingly arrive at his chosen goal or destination."

— Christopher Columbus

I must have stared at the coffee cup for about half an hour that morning, just marveling at the fact that it wasn't real. It wasn't real! It had been a very long, internal journey to get to this point, and I was having quite a new experience of myself and the world. The body was breathing and my mouth was talking, but the I that I now knew I was was no longer associating with the physical body in quite the same way. What a trip.

My quest had started in high school when I tried to figure out how premonitions were possible. I came to the conclusion that there must be a connection or a tapping into something that made them pos-

273

sible. Upon reading *Many Lives, Many Masters* by Dr. Brian Weiss, I came to the conclusion that this lifetime was perhaps not the only one I was going to have. And upon finding the answer that I was more than this body, other questions came up and were answered. I was raised Episcopalian and roomed with a born-again Baptist woman who read the *Bible* every day. We had been great friends during our first year in college until one night I asked her a question: "If I believe in reincarnation, will I go to hell?"

She took a long pause before answering; then finally, she said, "Yes." My breath got knocked out of me, and I said flippantly, though still very stunned and hurt, "Well, let me grow two horns and a tail then!" I turned over in my bunk and cried silently into my pillow. How was it truly possible for her belief to be true? For her, maybe it was, but that was not for me. I wasn't harming anybody. I was kind, thoughtful, and not hell material as I saw it! I decided I was going to get a definitive answer to my question and see whether her truth was *the* truth. Polishing. Polishing. Polishing. The next day, I spoke with a teacher at the Poly Christian Fellowship and ended up studying with her every week for many months, trying to see whether the teachings rang true for me and made any kind of sense logically. Above all, I like to follow logic first and see where it gets me.

I read many books on people's personal spiritual experiences. (Please see the bibliography at the end of this book). They all fascinated me, helping me get closer to better and meatier questions that not only answered what the base of religions taught, but what truth really was. I wasn't looking for my truth; I was looking for *the* universal truth. My research also made me feel more secure that there was more than just this body and just one death. I felt better knowing that all this striving and pain and experiencing was not all *it* was about. Seriously, what's the whole point of having all of this if that's it? (Of course, you have your own answers to these questions, but I am just sharing my personal experience. Take these words as you will.)

Power vs. Force by Dr. David Hawkins crossed my path through my father after I graduated from college. Dr. Hawkins himself had an enlightened experience at a young age. His insights thrust me further into the search for organization in this world, and especially for an answer to the age-old question, "Who am I?" I went to see the Dalai Lama speak in his "Heart of Wisdom" talks. (*Surely he is not going to hell!* I thought.) I read Jed McKenna's books. His pointy stick poked into that question, and I ended up feverishly working out the answer to my own existence. I questioned *everything*. The Hindu tradition calls it Neti Neti, the self-negation process. It took me many years and lots of looking and coming into realizations and letting go of old belief systems, that were beliefs, not truth. I wanted truth—the red pill from *The Matrix*. I wanted to wake up to whatever the world really was. My thinking was, *Why have beliefs if they cause pain and keep you stuck in illusion? Illusions cause pain.* The truth was where it was, and I finally thought to let the pieces fall on their own.

Back to that morning at Joshua Tree. The whole class was up at seven in the morning doing a meditative exercise before breakfast, and I was lying there, my mind focusing so hard on my spiritual autolysis, or autolysis for short. It means self-digestion, looking and analyzing everything and writing down what is true or what you think is true. You keep going until you actually find the truth. You end up finding a whole lot of assumptions and beliefs that you didn't know you had put out there until you do this work. I was applying the best way I could the lessons from Jed McKenna's book *Spiritual Enlightenment: The Damnedest Thing*, and I was finally at the point of stripping away the last parts. I kept asking myself, "What am I? Am I that tree? No. Am I my toes? No. I am still me if I don't have toes." And up and up the body I went, mentally hacking off body parts, trying to figure out the me that was unchanging and forever. Everything is impermanent except one thing—I just kept not knowing what *it* was! Off the body parts came until I finally had only two items left: the brain and the heart. I kept at it, tossing between the two, and after about ten minutes of fighting it, and fighting the fear that kept rising up about losing "myself," and what I would perhaps become or not be, I came up with a new tactic. I finally looked at this experience and conflict objectively. "If I'm not my toes, legs, hips, skin, lungs, hair, etc.," I told myself, "why would the heart or the brain be *any* different than those parts? They are all tangible and impermanent. They can't be any different." And then it happened—the realization and acceptance of the truth. Holy shit, it's *all* not me! The proverbial light bulb lit up and then exploded out of its glass shell.

Then I heard *whoosh!* in my head and through my core. In that instant, I got sucked through what felt like a wormhole. I felt like I was pulled back through the center of my body for a million miles, yet I didn't move an inch. I was here, but not here. My association to the *I* that I thought was me was changed to the *I* that is unchanging, the watcher, the experiencer—the part of everything that is yet nothing. It was simply awareness. That's it. The movie *Being John Malkovich* pops into my head now, and I suppose it was kind of what the writers may have been trying to describe. Who knows, but what is important is that my riddle had been solved. After about twenty-five years of searching, the gateless gate had been traversed, and yet here still my body lay. On the floor.

WAKING UP

My eyes popped open, and I looked at everyone and everything, with tears streaming down my face. It was all *so amazingly beautiful!* It all took on a two-dimensional quality (and still does to this day, for the most part). When we were dismissed, I talked to our teacher and my good friend, Babaji, excitedly about what had just happened. He replied, in reference to my morning meditation session, "I noticed you went very far away." Yes, well, that was an understatement.

Words were coming out of my mouth, and it was a bizarre experience to have. I lost my ability to form thoughts, but my brain was still working, and my mouth was still able to spill out words. He said, "Just go sit by yourself during breakfast and just breathe and be calm. Just experience." Okay. I gathered my food and my coffee, sat down at a table outside overlooking the desert, and just sat. And thought nothing. It was just still, calm, and peaceful. And I stared at my cup—which didn't exist.

"Reality is merely an illusion, albeit a very persistent one."

— Albert Einstein

Suffice it to say, experiencing the next few weeks was interesting. Talking was difficult because I was no longer connected to the words coming out of my mouth. Breathing felt like an unnecessary experience but still needed for the body to keep going. I kind of had to relearn how to be a human and trust that the body already knew how to do what it did. It allowed me to look back at my whole life and see the body's experience was truly a character in a play.

"All the world's a stage,
And all the men and women merely players….
Last scene of all,
That ends this strange eventful history,
Is second childishness and mere oblivion,
Sans teeth, sans eyes, sans taste, sans everything."

— William Shakespeare

A few others in Mystery School apparently had this experience and shared their stories of transitioning with me, giving me bits of advice, such as, "Don't get caught up in the experience. It is what it is." I heard that, but I was just so relieved to be finally solving life's big question and getting to the other side.

One colleague literally couldn't talk for two weeks after her experience. Another I met through NLP sat at lunch with me a year later (we were both staffing at the time) and told me that she had a hard time relating to people the same way after her experience. She told me that she no longer feared death and that life was just different. I instantly knew exactly what had happened to her, and I asked, "Isn't driving weird now?" She looked up quickly, realizing that I had gone through it, too. See, your depth perception is skewed because the experience of everything is in two dimensions. It was that way for me, at least. For about a month, I constantly had to look at the speedometer and count the seconds to try to stop at the right place at the stoplight. My perception was different, so I had to learn to get back into rapport with my body and with what my brain and muscles already knew. I had to trust.

"In that moment of realization your mind stopped thinking and you knew and felt beyond an intellectual logic. You perceived something directly in a way that transcended word descriptions. It is the kind of knowing that makes you look at the world, or yourself in a brand new way. Those little awakening experiences are moments when our previous assumptions or belief paradigms burst."

— Gary van Warmerdam, pathwaytohappiness.com

It's funny how once you have arrived at a new place, people come out of the woodwork and welcome you to the club. Who knew there were so many around who had gone through the same experience? It's not like anyone posts a sign saying, "Enlightened experience possible here." Some instead say, "Wake up!" Into what? Into your body. Okay. Into your heart. Sounds good. Be more present. Sure. But this? Why talk about a fully-embodied experience when someone is just getting in touch with her feet?

Why don't more people talk about what enlightenment is and what it feels like? For the longest time, when I read about it, I kept hearing the word "nothingness," and my critter brain went into overdrive protecting its existence. As I pondered the concept further, no-thing-ness translated to more of a non-tangible thing. It then became more palatable to my system.

For those seekers of enlightenment, I offer this: Once you have reached that experience: 1) It's hard to describe because there are no words that are useful in doing so, 2) It is hard for others to relate to, and 3) It's something most people aren't really interested in knowing about. They don't necessarily want their existence challenged, as you have learned before. This is your path to grow from, but not necessarily to thrust upon others. They are having their experience, and you are having yours. And bless all those here, doing what they need to do, in the ways they do it.

This whole enlightened experience thing, it's not something you necessarily bring up at dinner parties, unless you have had lots of wine and know people wouldn't believe you anyway—or perhaps they'll think you told a fantastic story, only to be forgotten during that night's deep slumber. They say, "Wow, cool!" and then move onto the current gossip which is juicy and truly riveting to their critter brains. Some may bite, but it's rare, so I have learned to offer it when it is useful.

"But when that which is perfect is come, then that which is imperfect shall come to an end. When I was a child, I spoke as a child, I understood as a child, I thought as a child; but when I became a man, I put away childish things. For now we see through a mirror, darkly; but then face to face. Now I know in part; but then shall I know even as also I am known."

— 1 Corinthians 13:10-12

Once you have had an experience like that, it is difficult to be part of things in quite the same way as before. Your perspective changes internally, and thus, the whole world looks different. What makes you happy now is not the same as what made you happy before. I do enjoy watching Warriors basketball with my husband, and I smile so deeply whenever I see my daughter. My love has intensified and resonates differently because I am more connected. "I am that, that I am."

Deborah, the head of Nine Gates Mystery School, shared with me that our brain undergoes what Jewish people call a divine marriage. The two hemispheres become better connected through this experience. And this state does not often last in quite the same way, with the ego taking a back seat, as does the body, feelings, and thoughts. It's just still—just being. Just awareness. Just noticing. Now. To stay in the now, however, does still require constant maintenance through meditation and doing what needs to be done. Some go back to the dream and enjoy it, some teach others, and some go further inward and disengage from society. We are all here on our own path, and it's perfect for each and every one of us.

When and Where Can That State Happen?

I heard one person had become enlightened while washing dishes at the sink. Buddha became enlightened under a Bodhi tree at the end of many days of deep contemplation, and after many years of trained meditation. It doesn't seem to be solely at the end of intense focus, spiritual autolysis, or self-negation. But certainly a giving up of what you thought you were, or being so aligned with the moment at the perfect place and time.

If it is your goal to become truly at peace with yourself, I would recommend reading Jed McKenna's books as part of your journey. He is clear, funny, concise, and tells a good story.

What Next?

The body will keep doing what it does. It needs to be fed, watered, exercised, and rested to keep going in good health. The body is already on auto-pilot, so just be aware. Enjoy the sunrise. Enjoy whatever it was you were doing before, unless you feel you need to go in another direction. You will know what you need to do. It will bubble up, happening as it needs to happen. For those things you weren't enjoying, perhaps the shift in perception will allow you to enjoy it now. Who knows? But I know the body and soul that I am experiencing has tendencies toward certain activities: gardening, drinking cappuccinos, dancing like a rock star in front of my mirror while getting ready in the morning, hugging, and playing with my husband, daughter, and dogs. In a sense, that stuff doesn't change. It's the you whom you identify with while all this is happening who has changed. The perspective has shifted, yet all the parts remain.

"Before enlightenment, chop wood, carry water.
After enlightenment, chop wood, carry water."

— Zen Proverb

Enso Circle. This symbol is of Zen Buddhist origin. A circle that is hand-drawn in one or two brushstrokes expresses the moment when the mind is free to let the body create. It also symbolizes strength, elegance, the universe, enlightenment, and mu (the void).

CHAPTER 17

FOLLOWING THE RIBBON OF LIGHT

"Do not take life too seriously. You will never get out of it alive."

— Elbert Hubbard

Since I was a child, I had always been fascinated with keys. I collect-
ed keys from my old diaries, music boxes—anything that could be
unlocked. It was thrilling even to think about what they would unlock,
what treasures could be found and enjoyed. The ornate handles,
dark bronzed finish, their unique shapes…. There is just something
that makes my soul wake up and vibrate with excitement when I be-
hold a key. A key has an aura of secrecy and is connected to something sacred and worth protecting. To be able to unlock something
that no one else can is both empowering and magical.

I think I first fell in love with keys while reading one of my favorite books, *The Secret Garden* by Frances Hodgson Burnett. It's the story of a young, orphaned girl who is brought to her uncle's house to live. She is offered a "bit of earth" in which to do anything she likes. He did not specify where this earth would be, so she deftly chose a place behind a secret, locked door, hidden away from prying eyes, where she could be free to create, grow, and dream. She had the only key, you see, and she intended to use it.

Every day, she wandered through the gardens, and when she knew no one would see her, she would end up walking behind the cascade of ivy to reach the door hidden from view. It was the key that allowed entrance to this private place, her sanctuary. It was where she learned about herself and about the world around her. She helped things grow, and in turn, all those things helped her grow, too. The symbiotic relationship proved to be monumental and profound. And when she finally understood, the garden was in full bloom, and she let the rest of the world in to witness and celebrate it and her. Like that garden, only *you* are the key to unlocking it all. You are both the garden and the key. Know that you are not alone in any part of it. You and it—it's all one thing. There is no separation from any of it! So the idea that you are fighting something out there is really you resisting the reality of what is here inside you.

The ego—as great a tool as it is for surviving *against* the elements and such—never wins in the ultimate battle. When armored with knowledge and knowhow, that little you fights to win. To win what exactly, it doesn't really matter. But winning some "thing" is placed at high value. The downside is that winning means someone else is losing. When you can place yourself outside of the rat race and come from a place of power, a place of non-judgment, and a place more of holding space and without opinion, a place of love, everyone wins, all the time. Every time. Why do people love the pope or gurus? To me, it seems it is because these people show no judgment. They are just holding your hand, softly rooting you to the ground again, and saying, "It's okay. No matter what you think you are, what you have done, how you think it's not working out for you, it's okay."

That holding space is so powerful because it is from the infinite, from love. Those who have learned to be in that and exude that through every pore of their "being," and have it translate from their aura for you to be part of, they are portals into the divine where there is peace, tranquility, and the endlessness of no-*thing*-ness. St. Francis of Assisi was known for his benevolence and kindness. Animals, being as sensitive as they are, picked up on the subtle energies of his lightness of being and were drawn to it. Many saints' bodies, after being buried for many decades, have been exhumed for various reasons, and their corpses have been documented to smell like roses, not rotting flesh or dampened earth. There is something magical that happens when one steps into divinity and is able to share it with others. Everyone wins and everyone benefits.

Oh, if we could only understand that our egos are the storyline we create, not the truth. The beings who can overcome their egos to be like the saints are few and far between because it is a long and arduous journey to let go of the illusions and trust and leap, arms open wide into the truth. We cling so tightly to that which we feel defines us, and in that clinging, we are caught in a tangled web of separation. And we view ourselves as small, separate, and fighting against one another. For what? Why? Because we fear the lack of self. But the little self, which is the ego and not real, needs to hold on to that reality because it cannot fathom being subservient to something else, or no thing. That fear of no-thing-ness is terrifying, but it is truly impossible for the Self to be nothing. Beyond the no-thing is the intangible essence of all that we are. No, you can't put it in a box. No, you can't hold it in your hand, but you can't do that with light, nor with a thought, yet those exist, too, don't they? Those waves of energy shoot through the universe at record speed, in no time at all. In the blink of an eye, almost—to be nowhere yet everywhere. That is the true essence of the holographic universe.

I wish for more people to become ridiculously awesome, *and* to know that they already *are* ridiculously awesome. I wish that they will know they are already so much more than they ever thought possible in so many ways. Out of the depths of our souls, when we really reach deeply into our greatest inspiration, that truth that is unshakable and uncontestable, that no one else controls by their egos, shines brilliant light out of our core and into the world—that brilliance shown forth is beyond measure and the only gift worth cultivating day in and day out, moment upon moment, pulse by pulse, breath by breath, all the time. When that focus and dedication and brilliance is not a doing-ness but a being-ness, you have arrived, my friend. You have arrived.

The ego has then taken a backseat and is understood to be a tool for the body's survival. The stories of your life are symbols for you to experience. Separation and fear ultimately teach the value that love truly conquers all, that people are just shells, that all "things" are merely illusions. In the movie, *La Grande Bellezza*, by Paolo Sorrentino, a sixty-five-year-old man's birthday coincides with his contemplating everything and everyone in his life. He takes stock of his life—the meaning, the absurdity, and the brilliance. In so doing, comprehension finally clicks, and he sees through the façade of his life and figures it all out. His last remark about this grand illusion is, "It's a trick!" and he smiles in fascination and awe. He realizes this life is the best magic trick ever! *This.* Obviously elusive and elusively obvious. The gateless gate. And it has always been right there underneath our very noses. The whole freaking time.

A FINAL NOTE

"I thought I was good after a few years.
After ten years I realized I was still improving."

— Gary R. Renard

Now that you have finished reading this book and absorbed it consciously and subconsciously, what has shifted for you? What are you excited about doing to make lasting changes in your life? How are you going to take the next steps into bringing these tools and lessons into lasting change and action in your life?

Let me just say this—no matter how many books you read, if you just wait on the sidelines, hoping for some magical change, you will be waiting a long time. I hope that this book has inspired you not just to believe but truly to understand throughout your entire self just how powerful you are. You are no longer trapped by the same old things you keep running up against. What has stopped you in the past has already started to lose its hold; now you are in greater focus of creating what you want. I challenge you to keep using the techniques in this book and keep breaking through your barriers.

REPLACEBECOMING RIDICULOUSLY **AWESOME**

Before you go any further, let's write down the ten actions you will take within the next ninety days. Maybe one is to let something go; maybe one is to iron out some long-standing issues with someone; maybe one is some small action items that you want to keep doing every day to help bring yourself back to center and calm. Whatever it is, write it down here and on another piece of paper. Work out the details and timelines of *how* you are going to make it happen. Go over the list every few days to see how you are progressing and notice what needs to shift in order to keep up with your goals.

Exercise

Write down ten action items you know you can commit to doing over the next ninety days.

1. _____
   _____

2. _____
   _____

3. _____
   _____

4. _____
   _____

5. _____
   _____

A FINAL NOTE

6. _____

_____

7. _____

_____

8. _____

_____

9. _____

_____

10. _____

_____

In this book you have learned about the many ways one can get stuck in life. We build walls from community and familial influences so that we feel safe and loved. This is how our brains work to keep us alive the best way we know. Overcoming the tapes in our heads, learning the power of gratitude, how to keep our center, and how to clear all that is *not us* from our daily experience—finding the power we never knew we had and being able to be more expansive—will help us be present every day. When you apply these simple yet powerful tools on a consistent basis, you are able to clear the cobwebs of the past and bring more connection to your highest self—that which you were meant to be.

This book has been a labor of love for me because my being stuck lasted much longer than I want yours to. Well, the time is now, and lamenting the past and remaining stuck for stuck's sake is pretty fruitless, right? You can truly make your life whatever you want it to be. If you start making your light bright, you have to keep it shining bright, no matter what. I hope that you are feeling more empowered now and are excited about your future with what you have learned so far. You know now that you have the skills, resources, and knowledge to make it all happen in just the ways you want. You just need to apply them and keep applying them even after you start experiencing results. It's your choices and your will that will see you through both the darkest hours and your finest achievements.

Please share with me your constructive criticism. I want to know what worked for you and what you would have liked to see more of in this book. What would you improve or expand on for the next printing? What would you include that you feel needs attention? I welcome any feedback you have. I need it. I want to help those who may have similar experiences as you. The more we share our experiences and wisdom, the more we can learn from one another and propel ourselves forward. Because my goal is to help and communicate clearly, you are a very important part of the evolution of this book's contents.

More importantly, contact me. Tell me your story. I want to know what your goals are and how I can help you achieve them. Reading books can be amazingly transformative, but sometimes we need one-on-one time to address situations more thoroughly and comprehensively. Contact me for your no-obligation, complimentary, thirty-minute life-coaching consultation via the phone, Skype, or Zoom. I want to help you figure out what exactly is stuck in your life and create a blueprint for how we can create a better life for yourself now. Tell me where you are in your journey, emotionally, physically, and mentally in all areas of your life, and I will do my best with the tools I have to help you.

Visit my website, www.ROIexperience.com, to read more about how to

A FINAL NOTE

make your life more awesome. Read stories, watch videos, and learn more about the work I do and how it can help you propel yourself forward in just the ways you want and need. If you want to hear me speak personally, to inspire and expose others to these awesome tools, perhaps you can book me to come speak to your group or organization. My cell phone number is 415-999-7675 and my email address is Meredith@ROIexperience.com. When you contact me, be sure to include your name and your time zone so that we can coordinate your complimentary consultation.

I hope you found what you were seeking in this book—and that you found even more than you thought possible. I hope you were inspired and encouraged by the stories and learned the many layers that create our experience. I hope that the many exercises have cleared some areas in your life that have made your life difficult in the past. I hope the tools shared are being implemented in your everyday life, and that you are finding lasting change and happiness in your world. Keep using them so that your life will become even more ridiculously awesome.

I am so excited for your adventures, every single one of them. I wish you presence of mind, balance of heart, and overflowing happiness in all your endeavors. Remember, dream big, hold on tight, and keep your heart open wide.

Fondly,

Meredith Herrenbruck

APPENDICES

APPENDIX A
BONUS: DAILY CLEARING

Just like we need a shower on occasion to keep our bodies clean, so do we need to keep our minds, emotions, and spirit operating at the highest, most refined vibration we can. Since you have learned in this book how your intention creates much of your reality, I have here a great clearing/alignment that my colleagues and I use often, if not daily. Say this in your head or out loud in a quiet place and a calm moment.

1. Clear all entities attached/non-attached that are negatively influencing me and my relationships with all others across space and time so I can have clarity with who I am and what I want to bring into my new balance.

2. Set my polarity to neutral. (Polarity means your magnetic balance in your physical body.)

3. Notice and release other people's attachments or projections of thoughts or feelings toward me, consciously or unconsciously.

4. Notice and release my attachments or projections of thoughts or feelings toward them, consciously and unconsciously. And my agreement with what those others projected (even un-intentionally) toward me.

5. I own what I created and let go of what is not mine. I take it back fully.

6. I acknowledge that others are not the source of my feelings

or beliefs, nor are life circumstances.

7. I take back all judgments and grief (and/or whatever emotion I am feeling at this time) that are others' and not mine.

8. I check in with any holes, leaks, or areas of depression, and I fill them in with my highest self, the soul part that feels connected with everything and everyone until I feel complete and whole.

9. I ground myself and center my awareness in the center of my body, just below the navel.

10. With a neutral mind and heart, I am open to receiving all the available and appropriate guidance to move through issues at hand, problems I see, in order to create with more conscious and positive action that which I desire.

APPENDIX B
COLOR PSYCHOLOGY AND ASSOCIATIONS

Red

Red is the color of fire and blood, so it is associated with energy, war, danger, strength, power, determination, passion, desire, and love.

Red is a very emotionally-intense color. It enhances human metabolism, increases respiration rate, and raises blood pressure. It has very high visibility, which is why stop signs, stoplights, and fire equipment are usually painted red. In heraldry, red is used to indicate courage. It is a color found in many national flags.

Red brings text and images to the foreground. Use it as an accent color to stimulate people to make quick decisions; it is a perfect color for "Buy Now" or "Click Here" buttons on Internet banners and websites. In advertising, red is often used to evoke erotic feelings (red lips, red nails, red-light districts, "Lady in Red," etc.). Red is widely used to indicate danger (high voltage signs, traffic lights). This color is also commonly associated with energy, so you can use it when promoting energy drinks, games, cars, and items related to sports and physical activity. Red has been shown to raise blood pressure and speed respiration and heart rate.

Light red represents joy, sexuality, passion, sensitivity, and love.

Pinkish-red signifies romance, love, and friendship. It denotes feminine qualities and passiveness.

Dark red is associated with vigor, willpower, rage, anger, leadership, courage, longing, malice, and wrath.

Brown

Since brown is the color of earth, it suggests stability and denotes masculine qualities. It encourages a strong sense of belonging and physical comfort. It is friendly, approachable, and denotes qualities of industriousness and reliability.

Orange

Orange combines the energy of red and the happiness of yellow. It is associated with joy, sunshine, and the tropics. Orange represents enthusiasm, fascination, happiness, creativity, determination, attraction, success, encouragement, and stimulation.

To the human eye, orange is a very hot color, so it gives the sensation of heat. Nevertheless, orange is not as aggressive as red. Orange increases oxygen supply to the brain, produces an invigorating effect, and stimulates mental activity. It is highly accepted among young people. As a citrus color, orange is associated with healthy food and stimulates appetite. Orange is the color of fall and harvest. In heraldry, orange is symbolic of strength and endurance.

Orange has very high visibility, so you can use it to attract attention and highlight the most important elements of your design. Orange is very effective for promoting food products and toys.

Dark orange can mean deceit and distrust.

Reddish-orange corresponds to desire, sexual passion, pleasure, domination, aggression, and thirst for action.

Gold evokes the feeling of prestige. The meaning of gold is illumination, wisdom, and wealth. Gold often symbolizes high quality.

Yellow

Yellow is the color of sunshine and is associated with joy, happiness, intellect, and energy.

Yellow produces a warming effect, arouses cheerfulness, stimulates mental activity, and generates muscle energy. Yellow is often associated with food and in general is great for attracting attention. Taxicabs are often yellow for this very reason. When yellow is too bright or intense, babies cry more in yellow rooms and more fights occur. Yellow can agitate the nerves. In chromotherapy, yellow is believed to stimulate the nerves and purify the body. Use yellow in moderation and hue to evoke pleasant, cheerful feelings.

Green

Green is the color of nature. It symbolizes growth, harmony, freshness, and fertility. Green has a strong emotional correspondence with safety. Dark green is also commonly associated with money.

Green has great healing power. It is the most restful color for the human eye; it can improve vision. Green suggests stability and endurance. Sometimes green denotes lack of experience; for example, a "greenhorn" is a novice. In heraldry, green indicates growth and hope. Green, as opposed to red, means safety; it is the color of free passage in road traffic.

Use green to indicate safety when advertising drugs and medical products. Green is directly related to nature, so you can use it to promote "green" products. Dull, darker green is commonly associated with money, the financial world, banking, and Wall Street.

Dark green is associated with ambition, greed, and jealousy.

Yellowish-green can indicate sickness, cowardice, discord, and jealousy.

Aqua is associated with emotional healing and protection.

Olive green is the traditional color of peace.

Blue

Blue is the color of the sky and sea. It is often associated with depth and stability. It symbolizes trust, loyalty, wisdom, confidence, intelligence, faith, truth, and heaven.

Blue is considered beneficial to the mind and body. It slows human metabolism and produces a calming effect. Blue is strongly associated with tranquility and calmness. In heraldry, blue is used to symbolize piety and sincerity.

You can use blue to promote products and services related to cleanliness (water purification filters, cleaning liquids, vodka), air and sky (airlines, airports, air conditioners), water and sea (sea voyages, mineral water). As opposed to emotionally warm colors like red, orange, and yellow, blue is linked to consciousness and intellect. Use blue to suggest precision when promoting high-tech products.

Blue is a masculine color; according to studies, it is highly accepted among males. Dark blue is associated with depth, expertise, and stability; it is a preferred color for corporate America.

Avoid using blue when promoting food and cooking because blue suppresses appetite. When used together with warm colors like yellow or red, blue can create high-impact, vibrant designs; for example, blue-yellow-red is a perfect color scheme for a superhero.

Light blue is associated with health, healing, tranquility, understanding, and softness.

Dark blue represents knowledge, power, integrity, and seriousness.

Purple

Purple combines the stability of blue and the energy of red. Purple is associated with royalty. It symbolizes power, nobility, luxury, and ambition. It conveys wealth and extravagance. Purple is associated with wisdom, dignity, independence, creativity, mystery, and magic.

According to surveys, almost 75 percent of pre-adolescent children prefer purple to all other colors. Purple is a very rare color in nature; some people consider it artificial.

Light purple is a good choice for a feminine design. You can use bright purple when promoting children's products.

Light purple evokes romantic and nostalgic feelings.

Dark purple evokes gloom and sad feelings. It can cause frustration.

White

White is associated with light, goodness, innocence, purity, and virginity. It is considered to be the color of perfection.

White means safety, purity, and cleanliness. As opposed to black, white usually has a positive connotation. White can represent a successful beginning. In heraldry, white depicts faith and purity.

In advertising, white is associated with coolness and cleanliness because it's the color of snow. You can use white to suggest simplicity in high-tech products. White is an appropriate color for charitable organizations; angels are usually imagined wearing white clothes. White is associated with hospitals, doctors, and sterility, so you can use white to suggest safety when promoting medical products. White is often associated with low weight, low-fat food, and dairy products.

Black

Black is associated with power, elegance, formality, death, evil, and mystery—even ideas! Wear black if you want to absorb more ideas. It is the embodiment of all color.

Black is a mysterious color associated with fear and the unknown (dark nights and lack of visibility). Black denotes strength and authority; it is considered a very formal, elegant, and prestigious color. In heraldry, black is the symbol of grief.

Black gives the feeling of perspective and depth, but a black background diminishes readability. A black suit or dress can make you look thinner. When designing for a gallery of art or photography, you can use a black or gray background to make the other colors stand out. Black contrasts well with bright colors. Combined with red or orange—other very powerful colors—black provides a very aggressive color scheme.

APPENDIX C

CONNECTING WITH CHAKRA WISDOM

Another way we can check into our experience and what is still stuck is by looking into the chakra system. These spinning wheels or disks are located along the spine and are psychic generators of the auric field. They are located near the seven major ganglia that radiate from the spinal column. Although there are some traditions that have five, seven, or twelve chakra systems, for the purpose of this book I am going to stay with a nine chakra system. Anodea Judith, Ph.D., in Wheels of Life says, "Chakras are organizing centers for the reception, assimilation, and transmission of life energies…[they] form the coordinating network of our complicated mind/body system." There are many more chakras in our systems than just the nine main ones, but for the purposes of this book, studying and working with these nine will be more than enough to start helping you to break through what is stuck in your body.

Judith goes on to say, "Each chakra we encounter is a step on the continuum between matter and consciousness." Similar to how our mind develops in relationship to the Reichian organismic rights (remember Chapter 3?), the successful care and experience of each chakra builds upon the success of the previous, from physical matter transcending upward into the more spiritual. However, when the lower half of the chakras gets interrupted, the corresponding upper chakra will compensate. The relationships are as follows. 1:8, 2:7,

3:6, 4:5. The ninth chakra is unaffected here as it is outside of the body. That means if the root chakra gets interrupted, then the crown chakra will be more strongly, almost hyper, developed. Blocked energy in one or more of our nine chakras (not to mention in our cells and organs!) can often lead to illness, so it's important to understand what each chakra represents and what we can do to keep this energy flowing freely and positively.

1. **Root Chakra:** Associated with survival. Associated with adrenals. Color: Red, Element: Earth.

   Represents our foundation and feeling of being grounded.

   - Location: Base of spine in tailbone area.

   - Emotional issues: Survival issues such as financial independence, money, and food.

2. **Sacral Chakra:** Associated with emotions and sexuality. Associated with kidneys. Color: Orange, Element: Water

   Our connection and ability to accept others and new experiences.

   - Location: Lower abdomen, about two inches below the navel and two inches in.

   - Emotional issues: Sense of abundance, wellbeing, pleasure, and sexuality.

3. **Solar Plexus Chakra:** Associated with personal power, will, and self-esteem. Associated with the pancreas. Color: Yellow, Element: Fire

- Location: Upper abdomen in the stomach area.

- Emotional issues: Self-worth, self-confidence, self-esteem, control in our lives.

4. **Low Heart Chakra:** Clinging Love

   - Location: Center of chest just below the heart.

   - Emotional issues: Envy, clinging.

5. **High Heart Chakra:** Expansive Love. Associated with thymus. Color: Green, Element: Air

   - Location: Center of chest just above the heart.

   - Emotional issues: Love, joy, and inner peace.

6. **Throat Chakra:** Our ability to communicate. Influences the thyroid gland. Color: Indigo, Element: Sound

   - Location: Throat.

   - Emotional issues: Communication, self-expression of feelings, and the truth.

7. **Third Eye Chakra:** Our ability to focus on and see the big picture. Associated with pineal Gland. Color: Violet, Element: Light

   - Location: Forehead between the eyes (also called the Brow Chakra).

   - Emotional issues: Intuition, imagination, wisdom, and the ability to think and make decisions.

8. **Crown Chakra:** The highest chakra represents our ability to be fully connected spiritually. Associated with pituitary. Color: Gold/White, Element: Thought

   - Location: The very top of the head.

   - Emotional issues: Inner and outer beauty, our connection to spirituality, and pure bliss.

9. **Transpersonal Chakra:** The highest chakra represents our ability to be fully connected spiritually. Color: White

   - Location: A few inches above the crown.

   - Emotional issues: Inner and outer beauty, connection to spirituality, and pure bliss.

APPENDIX D

KABBALAH—TREE OF LIFE DIAGRAM

The Tree of Life is a road map of one's personal development through human consciousness. It has existed and been used for thousands of years. This beautiful analogy of the tree, with roots, trunk, and branches guides you on your journey by way of seven stages of initiation. Rev. Megan Wagner, Ph.D., who wrote Awakening with the Tree of Life: 7 Initiations to Heal Body, Soul, and Spirit, explores these initiations in beautiful detail, while weaving in stories, exercises, and other traditional wisdoms to complement and reinforce the teachings. She has given permission to reproduce the diagram below for your use. The stages of initiation are body, instincts, community, identity, truth, transformation, and wholeness. The metaphor of the tree is explored in three parts. The roots exist in the bottom part of the diagram and corresponds to stages 1, 2, and 3 and "attends to the body and early emotional development." The trunk corresponds to stages 4 and 5 where one establishes individuality and develops personal power and one's truth. The branches correspond to stages 6 and 7 by "addressing our need to transform, renew, and widen our vision of life."

When overlaid on the body, MALKHUT (body) is just below the spine, YESOD (Foundation/Ego) is at the Root Chakra (base of spine), KETER at the crown (top of the head). The hips sit at HOD (Communication) and NEZAH (Instincts), BINAH (Understanding) and HOKHMAH (Wisdom) at the shoulders, and TIFERET (Truth) is at the Heart and DAAT (Knowledge) is at the Third Eye. Megan describes in her book that when we cannot successfully digest emotional energy from the outside world or even internally, there is a build-up of those energetic toxins, and that build-up can play out in the body. This diagram can be helpful for discovering what to process and then to release the toxins being stored. To follow the tree metaphor, if a branch is not properly supported by the trunk and even more, the roots, then it will show signs of stress. If you heal and make more vibrant the base of the tree, the branches will flourish more easily.

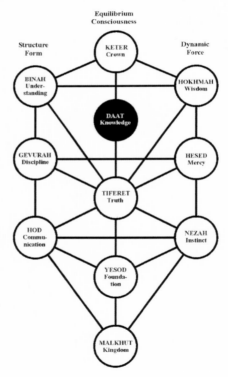

BIBLIOGRAPHY:
BOOKS I LOVE

If you are looking for more wisdom in books, here are some I highly recommend.

Burnett, Frances Hodgson. The Secret Garden.
Cameron, Julia. The Artist's Way: A Spiritual Path to Higher Creativity.
Chapman, Gary. The 5 Love Languages.
Hawkins, David R. Power vs. Force.
McKenna, Jed. Spiritual Enlightenment: The Damndest Thing.
Melville, Herman. Moby Dick.
Monroe, Robert. Journeys Out of the Body.
Nisardgatta, Maharaj. I Am That.
Pirsig, Robert. Zen and the Art of Motorcycle Maintenance.
Pollan, Michael. A Place of My Own.
Rand, Ayn. Atlas Shrugged.
Rocha, Adriana and Kristi Jorde. A Child of Eternity.
Schucman, Helen. A Course in Miracles.
Seuss, Dr. Oh the Places You'll Go.
Weiss, Dr. Brian. Many Lives, Many Masters.

ABOUT THE AUTHOR

Meredith is an author, professional keynote speaker, transformation-al life coach, and kahuna. Meredith studied at Nine Gates Mystery School in 2002, which was started by Gay Luce and is continued by Deborah Jones, and she occasionally staffs there when she can. She has studied at Psychic Horizons, an offshoot of the Berkeley Psychic Institute, to hone her intuition further. She has studied with Kahu Mark Saito over the course of three years, learning about Hawaiian spirituality and healing through the Huna Practice. She has studied at NLP Marin and obtained her Master NLP Practitioner Certification in 2010.

Born in San Mateo, California, Meredith grew up in Northern Cali-fornia as the youngest of three with two older brothers. She grew up playing in the dirt, sailing, keeping a garden, riding horses, playing tennis, and indulging in her love of photography; she continues with all those passions to this day. Time in Montana played an important part for her as well. It was enjoyed during breaks and summers, where fly-fishing, painting barns, fixing fences, driving tractors, and herding cattle were an everyday affair. Her favorite time there was watching the thunderstorms.

After graduating from California Poly State University in 2000 with a Bachelor of Architecture, Meredith worked at prestigious firms in San Francisco: Gensler, BAR Architects, and Andrew Skurman Ar-chitects until she decided to strike out on her own. During that time, she also began taking NLP and Huna classes to fill her curiosity about the unknown and the sources of her premonitions. She now shares her wisdom with others through lectures, retreats, and one-on-one sessions.

Meredith has always had a passion for helping others, and she enjoys empowering others by teaching them how to let go of their pasts and embrace their futures. Although she had challenges growing up, they have only made her stronger and inspired her to keep learning more and sharing her knowledge. She can relate well to others' struggles, and she supports people in all the ways she can.

Meredith is mother to a young daughter and wife to an amazing husband. They have two dogs and two chickens, a big garden, and live in a 1908 newly renovated craftsman home in Marin County, California.

BOOK
MEREDITH HERRENBRUCK
TO SPEAK AT YOUR NEXT EVENT

Finding just the right person to speak to a group of people can be a tall order, but if you want someone engaging with knock-your-socks-off stories, look no further! Not only will your audience and colleagues enjoy amazing stories and wisdom, but they will come away with a greater sense of empowerment and excitement for their futures.

No matter whether you are in Northern California or anywhere else in North America, Meredith can create and deliver just the right message for your meeting or conference. She knows that audiences do not want to be bored listening to a monologue but to be engaged and inspired with humor and wit and to come away having experienced and been part of something special and unique.

To see a highlight video of Meredith Herrenbruck and to book her for your next meeting, please visit her website at the address below. You can then contact her by phone or email to schedule a complimentary pre-speech phone interview:

www.ROIexperience.com
meredith@ROIexperience.com
mobile: 415.999.7675